CARLOS LARA

LIKE BISMUTH WHEN I ENTER

WINNER OF THE NIGHTBOAT POETRY PRIZE

NIGHTBOAT BOOKS

NEW YORK

ISBN: 978-1-64362-019-0

Cover art by Carlos Lara
Design and typesetting by Kit Schluter
Text set in Fjalla One and Bembo

Cataloging-in-publication data is available from the Library of Congress

Nightboat Books
New York
www.nightboat.org

LIKE BISMUTH WHEN I ENTER

CONTENTS

for my grandfathers

Hay un lugar lejos de toda ciudad. No hay un cielo sino varios, superpuestos, espejeantes, horribles.

¿Qué significará el amanecer para quien no conoce sino la noche y el sueño que sucede al sueño?

Despegar los párpados significa morir, desprenderse de una estrella. El ritual es breve, la entrega absoluta. Se grita con los ojos cerrados, empapado de sudor o crujiendo de frío: te amo porque tu latido ocasiona catástrofes, huracanes, guerras.

Te amo porque te bañas en un inmenso vacío y te alimentas de tinieblas. Nado en tus redondas pupilas ciegas como en un estanque infernal.

Tus propiedades no tienen número y abundan las especies innominadas, estériles pero eternas.

Te amo porque eres una ficción malvada y saludable. Si cesaras se extinguiría mi existencia de inmediato. Te podría hacer desaparecer en un abrir y cerrar de ojos. Pero luego ¿cuál sería el castigo?

BLANCA VARELA

Then they saw my name first where it originally was inside my head. In fact I've been told they may have put it there. Scopolamine thin shell for later for this.

CLARK COOLIDGE

QUAALUDE

so golden Aztec grief, headless sky of Jacob Riis, farcical nominalism,
the dream that eats your steak-frites for you, it all prays to me, all
what it was, some moments imbued with the crass economy of self,
some fragmented along the journey like shrapnel of conscience, the
deep dead-death etiquette, against the efforts of the misguided, but I
believed, in all respects and none, in the karma of the saint

> (in the precious car wash chemistry)
> (in the envelope of tears)
> (in the derelict barber)
> (in the transmuted capybara)
> (in the ketamine calendar)
> (in the tribulations of fake postmortems)
> (in the pervert's catamaran)
> (in the destiny of Chinese tongues)
> (in the hierarchical salmon salad)
> (in the rectum's tambourine)
> (in the cascading purple popcorn)
> (in the witnesses of chartreuse pie)
> (in the coldest tectonic flame)
> (in the salted beauty)
> (in the savior of rum)
> (in the first aviary underwear)
> (in the cackling syrup of revenants)
> (in the mountain's ass)
> (in the blue voice)
> (in the frayed and unconscious whiplash)
> (in the premium lull of magnetic thrash)

CERULEAN RODEO

Transient defibrillation of quotidian slur mentality with
blood bucket

•

Depaginated hearing persona as fourth sun or fire's warp and
mbira nebula

•

Deregulated suggestion of weather's amanuensis in a wig between
winter and winter's cream

•

Neutering symphonic verve with a looking bounty or beautiful
Venn diagram death

•

Unusual depiction with tungsten interior and myriad of poplars
in the tongue of light

•

Recuperative monitoring systems for emptied Aquarian blobs versus
the dark web

•

Paginated diffraction as exact bleeding feat as unblessed sky's
driveway druid

•

Defragmented conduction to sever palaver in discreet splendor with
maple syrup

•

Substantiated spastics versus designated brain key in substandard housing projects

•

Translucent lecture on choler and the vertiginous kitchen within a turquoise bosom

•

Resourced mnemonics and European blow-up dolls or else a butcher blow-drying the fauna

•

Clandestine trigger of chance surgical dispensation with acorns of light big enough to breathe

•

Proliferating perforation of the clinical layer of crows on Crow Beach

•

Connected triangulars within some exemplary she-male phantasms or mylar balloons

•

Triangular castration like immotile ocular theology or whatever slow scene corrodes

•

Patterning of the unequivocal substrata of other people or other pellucid octagons engorged

•

Cathartic seasons of proactivity without nuanced burst or engineering wheeze when vegetal baths go blind

•

Proactive recuperative nomination in auspicious flash distillery and similar Varsovian suit

•

Nonsensical egalitarian ministry as means of purification of rubies and ice packs

•

Dehazarding strangulation for the sake of heat or French toast or rental car

•

Alchemical vortex fricative with reverse erotic lobbying of course meaning baseball tincture

•

Desensitized simulation elective or African architecture puddle with ruptured placemats

•

Derivative orchestral polemics by three-digit code and four falconers' words

•

Coalescing figmented mannerism in defense of immaterial savagery coupons cut from brass beings

•

Material for referential massacre or phony colonial equipment sandwich

•

The core of mnemonic juggling as surveillance by California sin or cashew butter

•

Breaching suggestive numerology without exposure to covetous comas that read through rose lenses

•

The signals of shuttling queries in regard to a mortal doorway or teaspoon in Saskatchewan

•

Suffering regions of temporal devotion versus North Star elliptical browsing of deified dumplings

•

Residual sublimity in a survivor's mirror squalor breach or blank black checkbook

•

Creative predestined wager on electrical polar bear experience with cranial torture pampas

•

Subliminal heart as subliminal purple searching for instance purple coroner caffeine

•

Subliminal divination origin as prevalence of general neon fronds fallen by the bare bay

•

Retroactive sentimental pivoting bona fide and caustic with sporadic thespian tort riddles

•

Supernal gravitational botany foregoing any metaphorical quinine pie a la morgue

•

Adrenal wind gestation for a purposeful cipher of tangerine pursuits and pussies

•

Towing pure automatism like a puzzle of black flames in situ forgiving white trees

•

The bridge of coronal reasoning and sparrow-deepening with macro-distortion is a living creature

·

Dislodging atmospheric variety and somehow producing zealous
totemic abuse tablets at dusk

·

Cerulean rodeo beyond a vestal conniption of spectra beyond
non-breakfast and black mass

THE NEW DESNOS

16
Zero? Siege if could recognize question Bronx angles
Seven dirts hard giraffes Hong Kong to drugs lahars coccyx
North Liberia Bank of America FCC my co-vagrant favorite giver   Be

Vain gifted text quizzes
Baby has captains CDs 865 Gods pee
Hi
Liz says Ok

IMAGINARY EULOGY

where were we again never seeing
in a gulag's camouflage or untrue oblong distance ablation
I'll have the salamander bowl hold the pigeon pâté
as murals distract me
and dentists on the perimeter or printable lake blue Peshawar lube
my tears don't get out lest I lose them
I've seen no such thing as white orally or in the pie of real gel real
   Gherasim Luca detaille
putting fire froth of course in the visceral lanterns in the journalistic
   voir jilt
supposing both desires keep their long labradorite schemes
   conjugating
the few veterans I knew the few dungeons of seaweed amputated door
   esperanza confetti for seeing doves doves doves come with more
so many kittens so much Myanmar in my way volt spillage in my
   soul music masterpiece
I'm on my way
Bonsall diatribe skullduggery
will the Buddha statues last on the terrace I tell you to open wide
slowingly
the patience of indelible palaver oxygen
the lightning of youth is a stab all at once
why don't you caress them a year apart
so much bad stuff is slated to stop so much cake and jewelry deployed
   in the hold-up
unintelligible child truth
god plumped you like a cowfish

like a medicine kept in the movies for corpses or candy boring
    comma good life
it takes a good number to wear the desert down
we're not the only lungs that happen to appear in the here fowl
we begin to drip on the glassy blue beams
the smell of fennel or hydrochloric acid come with more
your head is bald like a grocery store
how do you deal with the womb of people

LANDSCAPING

you reaffirm me blinking in a nameless elegy powder cloud or down
   of consciousness
rememberer of sunlight ennui within a vegetal tint of crappiness
what resolution rests the head the numb Serengeti of drool
blatantly approving of love and life
testament of what is found to be a purple mouth star spilling
you thought the fire was wrath bourgeois floss or empathic ornament
   turning closer to death
in rebellious preparation Brownian tricks writhing every way like a
   three-day weekend
pixelated life raft of self-hatred whose dumb tickling shame will
   lord and flow
forever like beef Wellington suffering or relaxation

NEON REMAINS

It will look like the world you left, but it'll be different. Between congru-
ent and identical there seems to be another class of look-alike that only finds
the lightning-heads. Another world laid down on the previous one and to all
appearances no different. Ha-ha! But the lightning-struck know, all right!
Even if they may not know they know. And that's what this undertaker
tonight has set out into the storm to find.

THOMAS PYNCHON

they could be roasting there could be ruins of motive theatrically
    tossed into frame the fun bandage syncope
it is nice in the vista of the cold air refrigerator a slice of the kind the
    fourth kind selecting minds of berber
making me and Jamaica room again making air control dear trick
    making samples sit in the business pile
hobbling there where governors will go where willpower lulls in the
    conservative buttons or buttresses
in the hall of bravery in the Fidel Castro literal sky the res judicata
    New Hampshire plum pie forever
a wall of mountains doing on the planet a drafting theme these arms
    like a Cajun bird a murdered pharoah
autumn struggling to heal the carnival of now and stopping to
    glitter up the little eternities for vixen vines
the negative whittle and vellum the giddy parallax of alcoholic
    lightness the rocket boosters kind but not too
first here is me in the fur then the reign host the bright saddle
    mollifying the past or just homeless masks
she looks back into mazes of day and fast and supplies move into a
    climate unknown to tar to Sicilian octaves
I am a snow defined by chlorella by dense animal blood showing
    stones to the shore and revitalized porn

circular pagination fires sacrificed denim stars and a shoeful of
    bramble or buzz trying to define the other
I was about to accost you for the silent lottery the point being naked
    Yukon seraphs around a huge hell
the stakes of the sand of course of course the wheel comes first the
    interest comes second you come third
you cannot fight me I am the month I am the real lights of war
    growing big conically in vast coal mines
and I am saturated with ice lunches to be fair I am living in an eagle
    permanently fucked in the eddying no
time management a crown of thorns a special indictment dinner
    party in Cantonese blue bankruptcy foals
disgraceful and poor sheared off at the tendons the ornamental tears
    the riot suck flagrantly vibrating halves
the sky has a lotta water the fly is about it the meager Persian
    emasculated dunes are just no good resurrected
luxury alone excites the parts the 100 parts of the lark's mucus or
    pardoner's wand whenever hounds die
sometimes I distract myself from all the knives of the Hudson River
    and life and I rise above myself of course

I took the crime upon myself in arks on water in tuxedo tepid wafer
    puffing corn chips in my prime mover
floating cunt of love love the heart of love the paper of my heart in
    Tabasco like a pelican's perfume bloom
a mauve insistence and Latin payload there are video things and
    right here there are fisted brooms for sure
deceased and dressed for shrubs brought back to life by overheard
    blue palaces by blue casseroles in regalia
to work on things in Maryland to have a cigarette or rectify some
    sort of odd bulimia page of no thought
the bear of the vacuum stares at what it is and what it is not trying
    on my Byronic hat charms via hostesses
billowing bold half I debate my fathers over air air in a tin cup and
    whistling charnel speech batter surmises
leaving you vicarious banes in surrounding shoes parentheses and
    parallels sweeten time back or bones darkly
Canadian standard thesis of matter my hands change hands in the
    real world of water tables of jumper cables
there was once a guy there was once an extraction and in the business
    oracles shit and figure viable transport
also water weaving cerebral pilots also foibles also folios wherein we
    study thin returns of municipal lightning

as satisfying as this dust work is you never had to choose among the
islets which deny a raven a marvel
I am you European blood-European of my blood my eyes facing
away and you hurriedly deny Djibouti
melancholic horehound symmetry insisting on peaceful peace by
querulous assumption of odd disarray
don't tell about the after-slaughter the perfected circular currency of
prisons for sought-after recognizers
sustaining leads of unenjoyment lulls the barometers imploding with
doves fraught with candied realm fires
the platitudes the pandemonium and nothing remains whole or
original with or without seas to corrupt
I am perfected assemblage the dire daughter of silicon and adventure
research scaled to diaphanous briar
I see power I see the day 100% inside of a milk scene my grand-
mother tongue leaf in flames for eons
I was once waste unappealing micro synchronicity I had been a
classical face a racist foam clenching koalas
my song now rips your rain it lives in your pencil fronds crazier
than a red pony which casual dreams hunt
being that unoccasional arms race a glorified spark sometimes
stopping intermittently to wipe out the grave

I find a new path by which to tease a standard simply havoc in the
    ballerina bush the common aisle innuendo
casual growth of blonde air whatever dies is between the usual
    performance or velvet bust or infirmary veil
July the 6th ashwagandha flowers in deposition in several proverbs
    talking to myself again ribcage gauntlet sky
red and more red in my colorless coma in my epitaph of a driver of
    Michelles there were spells to regain
beneath a grey ceiling my body filed away cold Asiatic and un-new
    with failure or police brutality buns
a twitching comes closer the shears of my shadow awaiting other
    paths not to realize bathing was devilish rye
there has been so much ash in that world to release an apex of situation
    to hesitate each day for great goblets
hermeticism only disguises real love so much about it I have to say I
    am nothing compared to desirable bison
no plush agonizer of small bells no reflective limb or lingo disturbing
    the faith in a hundred paramilitary pliers
to certain pedigrees I am annulled or bland for my courteous run
    arounds my imperial hot girl hopeless inside
and what have you done to bring forth the flower of the invisible but
    turn carnelian cadence into gold glances

soft mammalian waterpark stanzas I go my own way now stunning
   palomax beatific cranial kittens come out
khalif of the burning subhelix in memory it's like a lavender gas
   mask people will have to love it and it alone
a form of fathering prehensile tails that float like a demonic detail
   congeries for famous widows to reflect
at this humble desk of dusk of illuminations I illuminate the nameless
   rings of a barbarous bell tower pumice
but you see daylight moving into my eyes daylight as lie and
   misdiagnosed pentacle or drizzle within drizzle
fratricide in soundless sighs with disc and pellet our style is an older
   thing of simple slow dreams vanishing
scum from the round flame against yourself to purify the bedsong
   the blameworthy the germane freeway film
two beings go to live among the gifted flow of violence and now the
   voices putting villains into opulent brine
when can our balances of unreturnable sky scars levitate with the
   pulp ellipses with feral inspector dredge
onward the throning estrus of famed purples do my magentas upheave
   a pilot light or pulsate driftwood
your diet is now the long lung stochastic I hate my thirst a complicated
   useless spiral of dust but dissident

within myself that is not the real Vancouver whatever is this cunning
    draft of life minus the reminders of men
this meandering prologue this diet strife of white crosses on the
    amber sky whiling some tangerine wave away
seduction of my scathed and charcoal shoulder exhibition an
    ampleness of night terrors and misgivings
watching your sheared mushrooms a fear in the doctoral glove
    compartment with contraband mirror stuffing
October gloam you know me as a window seat as a wet seal ablaze
    with war and sweet dormant flutes
coming into being like a blank opera of brushstrokes my last figure
    my apple denied space my Harambe novel
the scene is one of blowing cold eras within a vast collaboration of
    destinies or drachmas or flair inconstant
awaiting zero saints facing the lyrical lows I am Edenic diluting
    oracles with alchemical peach puree and such
within the sun's collective whiplashed wings within love within a
    fashionable holy oak found by future fur
colliding with all the near death festivities dispersing the blue blood
    of every glyph in the heart-shaped coins
I take it all home painting you and your country of origin your
    symbolism is the cross of my stare my stool
my permanent wear of prostitution after a while you get tired of the
    dark don't you Michael no material

world behind me in the black shell of rainbows the nudity of
  fortunate stains touring the mud duck musical
the hatchery of limits a pollen a rift a dying self enchained to upright
  mathematical disaster and ennui
for all we know we are avoiding the whirl in the glass of desire in
  the frivolous market cancer connection
tenfold loveless Chirons I swear I am mad at a specific we move
  around in the cupola like two of you
woe to the snacks of war woe to the literally marred scrolls awakened
  by weight by the hours of mantras
a crumb a porchlight partings shavings sacks for the almond beauty
  the bouncing winds light upon god
I've gathered four wolves for the differing selves and I had to as any
  rock could come for London engorged
my wire slow to slough starry-eyed Cancun plummet the dice and
  the mohawks have nothing but friends
when you talk about dusk and the hero I know such white chiffon
  such anal iotas that speak to the blind
speaking by snow by ruined ruby wing until the year is a balloon
  here a disappointment yet yes numbers live

right right right right right right right right right right right right
right right right right right right right right
what comes to the eye haunts I want says the black child says the
blacker child behold a place to clearly fly
original cobra do the traffic or immobile history guy uncorrupted
tangibility chateau guy peony guy
dancing on the concrete of my face guy these whistles burnt the
stew this street of crocodiles guy
laughing on my urban germs under what saliva crazy haven sermon
have you unrinsed your gel guy
panoramic castle creator invite a situation stare at the woods love is
no such thing that thing exists guy
thinking about twelve tone theory bubble people thinking about
some son of a bitch with weird tissues guy
circus disco way down there Judas today saying baby I know the
feeling the dream cha-cha going skippy guy
the Penn Station girls all real and unearthly unearthing other poets
moving their vicious ashes around guy
but now one sitting in the falsehood of Glasgow one unfuckable
shipwreck rumor multiplying forces guy
in life there is a great way to wave off novellas I wish it was within
the twilight of former train conductors guy
in the liberating district of breaths without breathing you cut your
life taking talk out of pure Samadhi guy
and everywhere the phony opulent architecture says poetry is like
saying but listen this shit is owed to me

to prove to you that a certain imagination barrier imposter sum of
heavy handed salvos disconcerts my minor
benthic possibility of ravens of salt water of stereotypical Christ in a
caravan of passive storage artists
I hate the word you willed that blistering chairless coin that
bleached hole of several nights not even there
he says poems were the giant vagina believing constant strong parade
you're getting used to verdant
what business luciérnaga you explore the car insurance kites and the
moving forward queers the movers
for miles for the form of beguiling infallible palaver straddles for the
betterment of terrestrial sea fruits
my apple my zero remains in the perfect torpedo we rest like pure
gentlemen carcasses passing varietals
I understand the old pleasing beauties rebirthed through calamitous
stripe fights changed and condensed
through augmented invariable dance halls when 10,000 mental
delights fog the stadium with sturgeon
the grave brass embedded in colored pencil enemy drinks you feel
the flavors you feel the turning
music discovers you now it sanctifies all the dead ice with sagas of
good hatred so yearly and yellow
I take my time in Transylvania I breathe marmalade in Addis Ababa
now Lautréamont you come too

is this a formal Santa Monica cycloptic wainscott Bremerton veal or
    corpse list or Kemetic ice cube incision

trammeling gurney pea or Mr. Diffidence in elements of reticulated
    Pharisee hunch where is the new donut

my mom is belted and bloodletting van Gogh goggles with pierced
    and devilish wristbands a waste of doom

your trick looks warmer looks Dunlop tire field and delegates'
    shimmer craze or preeminent steer pomade

betting your wide risible surface your jubilant casements of African
    mine formality it goes further

where you was at when the magic goat got colder when the herring-
    bone bliss besmirched the future glow

staple of sentiment abbreviated casual fire alarm soda in perplexing
    codas of Le Corbusier Lexington Ave

wise her five first blurs her naughty regicide frame turgid by the
    little myriads of shame the pompous dew

what could one know of the ventriloquist what could one beknight
    but a lesser shadow coveting human grace

apparently grass clowns and convex machines apparently hymns
    from the Bhagavad Gita played with patience

I see no firm world in the rise of oneself I see no sun in the cool and
    sharkless mist mantra or hexagonal hurt

budding oneself with blood and Samsung electronics and Parisian
    groves with the overt risk of skirt steaks

I see a shape I see a yellow nothing formulating manure for nothing
    in the amaryllis mercury theater de novo

as the purposeless fuck in draconian lounge courage as the church is
    a clod of surfaceless lost racquets

a shimmering vibrates from beneath and a different store brightens
    the horoscope the small flowers for what

I am what is what when I am saying what I said the perpendicular
    ossuary the balanced collusion cues
I wish I could order a high rise online a malleable sensual Crenshaw
    in drops of arid light
Danish king medleys moving through hell on a matchstick put the
    sauce in the oven heartfully
send me something spray something in Panama crisp as the insane
    blast force of Liechtenstein
no new monologion no new merry cataract colossus in determining
    the trickle of awakening
and when I tried to say the most precious I failed and so disappointing
    to be trapped in space
endlessly derelicts with 60 eyes are sweet and adorable winter
    assimilation weirdness or peephole sophistry
this bottomless ground view this purple and flashing hamster for
    love is the easy life dishonorable
without a weapon without a hog-tied dividend parade my non-nucle-
    ar suspension of a spellbinding Sobin
I can't understand a word you're saying and I'm not afraid of the
    mink horse are you are you the solar fist

faced with my own epigrams I hover like the fluorescent white suit
  of truth for you and drop my palette
moving in the new pattern moving into escape itself so there is none
  the force of thought untranced so easy
she could be the chance of ruse the magic aquarium in spheres
  manhandling oval ivy until nothing is distant
dropping sun in Missourian paper tables take what is nonchalance
  aching with passwords or 20 souls
for five years in a white bull proving all the while the imagination's
  foundries medium Marquis elations of pop
gas prices ice what to do in the area the solid U-Haul iris Nubian
  hassle the fool moneying his populist Diana
turning gold into actually gold lmao I charge the air for its channels
  right now now you know everything I do
when I say what I mean I go glorious my eyes coast when the neon
  frost twirls alive like the deep South
all of love in my way all surfaces in the blended vacuous satyr's
  half-sleep of clover and scars' investments
why make this up why fortress why art class or Japanese gnomic no
  one making stuff in three dimensions
plain with the winter or summer plain life with eternal BBQ wings
  self-gods and we would never like your art
chased by space if I cannot write the bird if I cannot write weight
  my minivan and smouldering trillium tools
transcribing spells with Bill Gates or odds of the cloak's games there
  is very much vapor and stateliness in you
awkward velvet does not lend its hats to rhyme yet I await its response
  addressed to the demon I am in blue

do you fling yourself into the shitty ocean twins kneeling like some
 obsolete Angeleno moon blade
to stop arguing among three hearses to really feel affection for the
 moon otherwise a pre-precipice of strife
I'm slightly the bad guy sightly Baghdad supervising the sun what it
 means to be human or a drawstring
something that had to have been mostly the gestures filled with
 great cities when titular cornbread retreats
last of the flat-fallen forms of auteurism the lagging fire of omnipotent
 pawns sharing matters of sound flags
my eyes as victorious sciences after the vitriol after the parachute of
 the very minutes of all the guilty quails
I heard a bright bite be the Laura of bottled green be the wish taps of
 the mind in Cincinnati or Cirebon
you should not be able to be a monk in the special solvent in the
 emigrating hurricane of alongness
once a week this exclusive toboggan voyeur my Mexican-looking
 seeker stay back and glancing and amidst
be grave in the boring iron spring be visual as kept in a newer fulcrum
 of sleep be jade of the asymmetrical
while the walls weep I dissipate into this hook of metric fits the
 round flames of the portrait of round flames
blowing greenly into the yes the stand-alone eye fairy unconvincingly
 channeling ascension for perverted fun
this is the way it was while I was screaming becoming while being
 my aleatory love shape my arbitrary texture
and yes I love the world's ass yes I love the districts in which I close
 off what I am for another day or wave

I've been writing I've been even darker on the diamonds than I was
    before I took you in a spark of infinity
you'll call yourself the rain one day twitching for me like justice in
    the unsound rondelay of worldly tissue
my love is the ark of the wrong it is night out of disregard for you
    begin to see the voice of beryl birthed
my love for you is trapped ever in the chapel of its own speed leading
    me to dissociative Mississippis
the others are to go meddle in the affairs of the Eucharist unlike
    planetary circles of this sordid phony life
to unseat the roads of reversal in tears to lose a paradigmatic canon
    of the mazes broken by closer closeness
daily rips in the mind go forward as red honey expelled from life the
    yew of the upside down cakes of bonds
it's a different ball game now a nexus of new terrains are captured in
    a fatherless two-sided soil supermarket
the sky as fallacy as razor's edge as the home bums of Wisconsin
    man what is with the Jewish salad dressing
aced in aqua imagine aced in the panties door of resplendent sponges
    laughing at a casual party perpetrator
that used to be me right fucking there with a wonky right-there
    type of ghost that wasn't mine though
it was a dream too loud and unexplained for sick of being taken out
    of his little can his wife in the swear word
it's about what comes later in the drop it's what sees us as separate
    from a lot of the waters deadly waitress

I see no new comedy in the way I look at it as a foreign glowing a
  harrowing of what art is in skull
totally out of the fade he admitted anomalies of the whole the really
  jettisoned parts of deities
we're wasting our lives no doubt about that ensconced but lost like
  some kind of organic Kierkegaard
still grasping at a way to make the bed a more permanent thing to
  string up financial babes in paradise
she can't actually hang the gold or wear the dolls we live in other
  powers of closeness unwanting infatuated
auras don't leave the judicial sleep we're going to be way in Providence
  hunting pleasure at the villa
martyrs of the grey serene blows my aquatic cheddar my one-sized
  ring my hazmat alphabet under lovers
we don't bleed we barely look at the despondent air hotels still within
  the week still nicely in the snow force
most eyes are bereft of the penis most knights have an inner light of
  pause and garbage and summer cars
it is us as one now born now higher now stationed with borrowed
  muscle don't hold me so long
appropriately this music is candid Homeric breaking friends apart
  who come to the luxurious age of shrimp
no more drawing in the wavelengths there should be signs in the
  social praxis the compound business strategy
one malignant playground one phantom Brooklynite fitting the
  surreal within the jurisdiction of squirrels
once I imagined clearly the single suburban tampon in a feud of
  roses in the normal wings of sacrilege
and the taxis of orchestral matrons came with me and I was happy in
  the light of that happy

it's so like you to be uncrucified to be loosed upon the walking hoe
and velocitous oyster of all else
ambivalent stardust recidivist wandering over glib in the strawman
parish you zoom among grass
you net the living incest of the metric sun its quadrants solo in a
pungent matter a way is found
a luncheon of athanor a temple above the neck you are grey and
white in the swipe of orchards injuriously
measuring whips by magnetization having one long maddeningly
wavering like salt on the cusp or stunt
cold sphynx emporium whom have you bought with time if this is
your first wave this is the time
tracing two Olympic elements like a droll whale the suite of no
noise the Friday of all colors there is pure pain
like when we revived your chevron head your fat intuitive sanctum
your Jaime Saenz saying of every crux
of course there are satellites too unique for seasons for popularity for
the grasp of the golden door
elevators of ink open onto old children and what happens you do
not have Jesus in your heart girl
yellow milk yellow charcoal I want you on me in all the games of
gun nights in the sappy stirring of outcasts
diablos begin to question these me zones the something something
of comic books of French or Korean love
I've seen you tattooed in pink your little eyes predating nothing but
maleness or cortical valleys of throes
and then this life became the last thing to advance like the methods
of palm trees or else the idea of them
this is a deck of cards a high ancient actuality pouring the chimaeras
out of whomever at the end of the mind
the flashing lights have always been for those who qualify and the
horses of life are shot on sight forever

you whose barking shutters the ghoul quarries whose quays are
    enlivened prism feeders releasing dogma
I dream abroad in the imageless heart in the scoopy afterlife Marlboro
    Reds plain badgerer
sodomized feijoa commandeering fucking feijoa it all came back to
    me like that drinks many drinks
what is this hammerless excision Kabul pattern doing in a little
    jettisoned meat what about elocution
the guy says if the classics had a wide circulation the guy says fat girl
    terrestrial pterodactyl soup
oh my eyes warm burger fistulated evening journeys come to me she
    comes to me to warn me of Oman
but my tumors supply purrs and I mean that white man I mean a
    brief dismissal of Chateaubriand
baked organic crunchy pea snack the fertile public the nerve of reversal
    accompanies a charm of kernels
Cedar Rapids state securities guys aliment going nowhere neither
    Marlon Brando would do it
the wealth of the calamity of the René Char babies transitioning
    from found world to ape door
my performance to achieve the effects of life through all uncertainty
    of course poetry is not for reading
wicked in a way olive if you have what I don't I'll tell you about the
    mind in front of anchors and pearls
common to be the cause of god certainly the wild boat certainly
    authors will squeal into nothingness whoa
all day understanding the scheme of schemes she cried a little bit the
    plans were all airplane or blackface
the banks don't kid themselves kid everyone attempting to squeeze
    everywhere in a holy communion of .22s
translating Éluard on Ka'anapali Beach and where do the dead go
    feeble piña coladas of glamour's orgasm

I'm all over the floor and bothering you we don't have meat together
    air can't be hooked onto ponies
there's a difference between good Bali and me the tanks of desire the
    boil of the dead or transparency plots
there's a bitmoji guy a charlatan growing in my Winnetka helmet
    languid summoner lame banjo decibel
there are subconscious militant roads that are women lions and too
    bad you're stuck to your head
hold still mango the gold pulled out the second god don't fuck the
    unknowing donning Buddha's stairs
we got drunk and wished the world well my fire is people flavored
    Dali would see trees where I see dikes
don't let the pros happen money one life to which I actually say yes
    everyday those eyes and those eyes
the spread of surrealist layers above which he uh hanged himself
    each shell marks a flying disease gum
these little asexual programmatic punctuation marks will always be
    the better half of encores in Damascus
the flowers come that way and then they start to vaporize you too
    aren't you anxious to hear in the Linux
bodies backgrounded captured by pumice bodies unbound through
    horticultural mesmerism in England
I heard my wolf bachelor and that was enough heard the sod break
    into itself and say that's healthy baby

WHO LOVES PEOPLE AND VALIANT ART

oh bad and bad and bad bad / each peach tree arisen in the polis
each violent quill / remember these are not instruments of peace
remember the sun is all you'll know of Earth / destiny an afterimage
of chaos or cold stoves
pedestrian form blatant calendric moaning in orbit

be cautious thunder be slithering sister
and then you turn empty handed to archaic verdure

drinking wine from a seagull / I aerosol the day / baseball tomorrow
give me the skinny curse

or pass the expectorant
I have love for the fade of love
the world under the real world under the real world
real life true freedom

REAL LIFE TRUE FREEDOM

these petty things that drop their dilations
      catch masks and blonde ones in the wide fields
one or two avenues will pill the brush possums
      of my ghost church of rectangular deepening
like unharnessed Bolivian catapult figurines
      inattention to dick is an astounding goal
your grey pants your spattered cow hands
      festering womb goat ominous daffy shoot is a feeling
yes facing desire like tan and fiery coffee mugs
      are there oceans for viewing in dishes in kitchens
the apparent pee train the larynx as voltaic vaudeville
      by the living familiar Lorraine by the misapplied rose
gaunt with insurance premiums hysterical mocha
      at most the sea sprayed sparrow wins Lithuania in thought
golden nymph telepathy or injury on one mild man
      to the people I trust with data in my mechanical popcorn
you found the mystical husband hole
      the taqueria blouse with rose right in the oral tea
oh god that's good hurt yourself
      vexed kinetic raisin weeping or nightgown
say it to the yearly napkin refusal the Clydesdale
      carpet bombing affluent melancholy crab cakes
you don't kneel to punchbowl scenes of father
      you don't abide like a fatwah in marmalade moon shapes
sure penitent clay boy you think I killed my biographer
      your sick suits top the schematics of truth like a sylph of love
this is the scroll of her hair new swooning ungulates
      sure things in the rote minor destiny of the internet

two more modes for hovering shine dates
　　　　rapidly give therapy tumors to red floors
tell me something lovely or I tell of all the steaks
　　　　archbeast of the silent auction muck I discussed
teeth in a green bag
　　　　sheen of the awake government lung
a portal bleeding under whole writings
　　　　I take the fake winter wing beyond you faultlessly
mohawk motor stick when will items revivify
　　　　I spit on the stone of adjourned temple sofas
we killed fury for far less like no respect for stillness
　　　　see the vehicular rose the parsnip of Bucharest
tell me what can no demons rebuild then
　　　　what fire would shingle a reddened fuel blend for mercy
to listen to fervent Canadian vintage silently holding cards
　　　　it comes to claim me to annotate lust with capricious regret
exciting schedules ahead you know
　　　　despoiled calisthenic child marking the flood
musical weapons losing hope
　　　　wicker wild with crashing skulls with rose pieces
see the distant super fact of similar horrid meat
　　　　a cup of people mutual with VHS or the Belle Époque
freesia or conics in speaking of hot pedantic preternature
　　　　no ghetto or traffic arena for friendless bloggers
I reserve the right to call you out then
　　　　when the Bronco glass wipes you clean
a laundry of stones a dented iridium wagon
　　　　becoming the room temperature maiden flask
there's a principle for the corn mind coil
　　　　ignominious trees fly through yellow babies or bank vaults
as an untitled Wagner binder glows with mango mirrors
　　　　a proper teacup stall a germane quiet window
a finch releases all the fire from a dying traffic cone
　　　　envisioning your apartheid ring of influence once it engineers
architecturally ingratiated to the presence of half calamity
　　　　hollowed by time in its calculus of disgrace its balloonish
　　　　qualms

foreign sigh batter for unavailable margarine sulphurs
      defecating in the catholic flowers I see a blue summer a blue
      rising star
like the uninvented vitriol lunch where both of us explore a diamond handle
      and dispassionate road blood similarly

THE INFLATED TEAR

I see into people whatever a tree dormant and green doom
salivating hallways appear in concussive old me
what celestial car bombs desire a long cauliflower fire
you know the witch that came out of you
plural inferno of Gloucester of textual rampage bread men
sapphire headgear
Aucuba japonica inspirational demon tide and thingy
oh the place the person each tier of peerless wraiths rain with the
    vintage voice
intending crème de cassis as such equinox severance beautifier
oh friend and butler in the game of chairs and tights
purple fume in the desk and matchbox carnage counselor
telekinesis pleasures or light gummy flange of despotic tots
ruin the wall of pain ruin them all in pairs or pears

THE NEW DESNOS

Grand
"

Dear Judith, for dark heights, sleep.
"

Feel sleep circa 1223 – – effort is difficult and very phantasmal very
   very decent
lux power demonic episode
Hang for a second. Total fecundity evacuating your vial for the
   figments in cancer

Just I

THE NEW FEARLESS DEATH

yes yes
yet tables burn in fictions / what I found on my bed in Slackerville
American weightless meridian sigh
I hope a heroin addict turns up in your plasmic outburst portion
your normal and headless penumbra skitters away
today we are holy soft penetrating nothing special people
Jean Follain Coco they make life so beautiful so very beautiful again
I don't want to raise contradictions to comment to remark
I want to connect to weave to dream not interpret purely what is
this book this poetry this poetry will save us all / but when the wind fucks around
and the dissonant midget waning works / then owls then hysteria then
you understand this isn't a simple overheard aloha
I've been writing to the void aloha to return aloha with symmetry aloha
any science moves the trees to joke more than a significant Uganda
more than revenge in this Bellini's bottomless taint
more than alphabetic surprise or the bells swelling
no college or phylum no Autumn takes a towering death down
only brittle star only mattress of lambs only look
right here
a mirrored kind of Ulysses a Satanic Satan / these unright tweets
a snatching of galaxy whose ghost hiss reminds me of self
of course c'mon

THE SALIVATION ACTOR

*J'ai jeté quelques gouttes d'eau sur une tête de mort
et un mât de cocagne m'a reconnu pour son frère*

Benjamin Péret

I

The actor breeds spirit to numb sound. Probably a boat somewhere, a sad death thermal or opioid, positron. Little death, little numb malt. Slow time blends, human slobbery or frenzy. Hawks fizz in midair arousal slits. Emblazoned with chrysalis, ungodly god.

If a chain is a lung. Three broken beds. Succor the sky.

And then it's property. Penumbra access. Freckled villager, do drinks inhabit them blights. Roman coagulate spiller. Free crestline gore. Free body of granite and grape juice. Girls wear the force of laudable food. Breasts resplendent with undulant holiday steel. Cruising the fear, stellar on the doorknob. Flipped in the welted plumb, cannot act not head.

Pausing of the risk eye, calm first ball smuggling drums, I'll not worry about a Christ spume, I'll do what I can with ten colors. As a body goes awry, your body softens by the deal discs, apple of love and diesel lore. A source of blue, meat trestles invest kaleidoscopic blue breath, to prove excited renditions. Tibia in the breach, the world together like a sweet pox. What powers the needle powers the skimmed aerodynamic. All vats of Chicago, hooch, the penalty vestibule, tasting purview. I can have some malaprop at the Getty. Iridium bean with you, pretty blob.

II

Pure kirlian can, black in the waterfall field. Take your wrist and vein totally model. Rumbles, doctor lion, see my candy eye, swill the drawer a hailing, fear a blown away chicken muscle row. No intention for snow or vial or viable docr, blonde scream cake.

No more real time. Across the Vladivostok ladder, uric oral dot-com. Call it the hops, is that the one dirty bible. Is that the aspirin life, prophecy amor, all things have a drink. No one wants to know if the widow flies. Is she kind of talking to the place of the plum.

My fear is the ripped elixir. My striping is the seed of all that.

III

Octopus big tunes who are out here. I have heard the lynching you task to fumes, from affable future pharaohs, reductive purpose. Who are the tortoise flies, candy become. Liquid credit card veins to unlike the rivets, the movie of no precedent sea.

Stronger hock amen. All last days, they're plain lend. Circular goy fund, desire great grain frontage or humble cheval. Paladin stir, or ossuary syrup stir. It is the gallivant same. The peach reservoir with squirts of dense interstice vases. Only 2,000 words drift, valiant crease.

File cabinet sparks fill the June okra. There you go. Repulse a star. Control farm bashful speakeasy deepers depend. Alone algorithm distich treble. Where we made pale cages. When one thing stares at you, the rest is impenetrable barking crate. So suicide voles rebounce. Then leech peace to divine whatever simple seraphs. Whatever cat mouth. And which way did we always transfer. The lock votes upon a pee or bread. Picture that in a burning panda.

IV

Cloak vacation climb, but where in the fail-safe velour ischemia. Impenetrable chamoy but subspecies and florid jack water. To call it the vegetable of milestones or the clitoris jury and yet tremble as vesicles plainly play. The more capable plenary fruit or green fruit. The aluminum can of asses.

Non-composure. Feeling the bled blend. Or what other oracles say when juice is rayed. New time crumbles. And anything in the fat static defibrillator because I know in the chastised apprentice pool that kids rescind. Resin ago my payable purloined shower reef abides.

Fear as a cornfield or seatbelt quaking. Fear as a white window into wood. Fear as jetty or spoon billed catfish authorizer. Zero mechanics or poison Yukon session. A scientist, and when tree fonts entangle, where is she dressing the argon. Why policing corduroy or human sample stickers. What was an eye but a splendour. Coagulate aroma never sips a draft of itself. Hurricane lung Deuteronomy king's kiss. Without six tongues or without arresting glasses. Voyeurs who stash themselves with piss folds. In the bitch of a Karen cold, one lustre finds a terry cloth, the same empathy. A sphere calls on itself to be extraterrestrial. Of course, the cup is the friend. Bedrock and pineapples have found a way.

Old radiator, my delivered first empress peel. What lump sacerdotal is canister health. What geriatric mollified museum pile. I peel green up as it is all I see. I call umbrellas to your gastric voice. What darkness sleeps in the vestibular craft perm.

V

Okaying whatever mental staid drum. Whatever limbic demurrer penicillin. You can extort blue stars, sure.

The meister that incorporates family dead silence.

Wherever trees babble, blanket ceiling of industrial parts, Yucatan and narwhal enjoined. My ring elongating neon headaches. My pressuring sound vampire or vampiric pedestal storm. Microfiche phantom tongue, nobility sheds a rising flog, no cream in the parking lot burn victim's departure. Skin awakened translucence, perhaps an organ changes or a red gropes from Egypt.

You see, palaces don't, and swarm with smeared ear. In this wing, pain is a cube.

Little invictus hazard of the spell dram, orientally, but with one poulain. A sort of scope away from whelps. Grey fruity and shoe beam. Like places in woe sense.

A black bear and one vial, across the clam, winnowing TV.

V I

Alien query, vicious camp euphony. Spading a wolf to true sophistry. Afraid of the senseless whale stockings. History is a nation, lug by increment.

Pater nostrum bobble head, typhus dusk. Trees under caution, label gold shooting seas. Tundra, or dent in the wary monocle savor, to dominate a cocaine sand, invade the day. The tours that blame Eritrean ghosts for marble flooring, no more commonplace sternums, no angular weight tests. Ignoble sanskrit party with Haring woven into youthful pack alignments. The stars assured to hunt a skate. To redden the wolp. A carnivalesque gravity stanch.

Nevertheless true mongrels dream for iron. True surface must tensile pain ochre. Or spot Wiccan morsels off diaphanous tellurian games. What supporting possums claim as younglings in volition. Grain, explored, unguent Gallipoli torso or re-vast temple mortar. Purpled by the Jameses. Furnace cars await gaffling.

It's the chase of jury creeping into fever a dramatic Reverdy. The Aristotelian beaver comports with god code. Police fritter their batches encaged by Gurdjieff. For four themes in dew, for tethered falcon hugs lower than buoys.

VII

Abusive marsupial conduit body, nope, the goal of trapeze experience unfolds the dikes. The safety of flea market campfires. Will insert moves into the one. We will know everything sitting, the scabbard of tar, lowly frenetic puppets of bone. Shall.

Shallow mothered beans, across the sinister tangerine blood ball, scoops a jealous reservoir breathing hole. For you to be healthy in the plain, for great song gel killing, for umbrella graves that boost themselves over floods. A fallacy shown to divers. One fig from the flagrant craft. Exploratory genocide forgery capsule, romantically sealed in the skatepark from hell, or coagulation meddles with its wings. Superb ponies reduce themselves to an email address.

In a federal diagram choker, headgear responds, as a pamphlet of death's duty, as a cage where assault is unrehearsed. Consider the other parcels of sodomy. Consider stylistic panic from a merganser's pole. Consider the delicate floor flame. How it walks within the bells and spheres already indicated. Who propels a foolish game of unfurthering the yellow stationary eventual.

Beryl blue leaf, quotidian quiz, lift the rain of Kansas from a human purse. Repeat the teal skies like that. Osmotic replevin of the grey shine, dissonance in the real trials of turpitude. Cash and indecent plant photography. Natural plight of the scales in mourning.

VIII

Pure mantles of alien food. Pure chess lists. Indiscriminate slight tower yearning. Owl series of sensory thumb timings. *Ashcroft v. Iqbal.*

You learn about a patriarchal disc copy, a killed freezer pouring human heat from its polemical pie.

Of course imploring vermillion star custard one is never to become a paladin's chief kiosk.

One is exploratory in business dew, otherwise dreams jail an anchor or anchovy. Where in the solarium's sedative claim does it hubris or apple pie. Whatever notion gorges politicize, abandoned fruit snacks, arterial garbage dream. Canadian dream of human bonus triage. A muezzin. A material breach. Corporate syncretism.

An osteopathic estuary in the middle of dying. But what did the material say about orphanhood?

IX

Maniacal hose per se. Otolith. Parameter of eggs and teeth. All eggs and teeth. As soon as a fall residue receives itself, there will be ground and red fog. Troves, impassive police dithering, or Palestine verifying huts for kinetic vitriol nuisance. It seems what tiny panthers implore.

Bright grey dream denim miniaturizing the ferry room. The ruinous ablation of dates. The champagne severity of a plain sky's cry removes. No polyphony to co-vasculate.

I said no polyphony to co-vasculate. A serum of boring chairs. Birds chirp.

X

The wedding of radium, loosely agate or poor babies, something goes on. A star is parked, a storm prances. Various cornucopias enter a jasmine as entrance flows directly unusual or yellow bows pile up off-kilter diadems. Never more estrus than harm's harp can occlude. Futile car passionate or Juvenal's verdigris schedules, whatever borealis camera pole. Nom de plume.

Several of the markets begin. In my breast or my breath niggling tortoise sculpture, window water, Appalachia tries. Larynx fondue, you hum the quibbles of unfounded digital masonry. Lucky igloo, burst wafer monocles, or a kaleidoscope of kale's hungry hairbrush. Teardrop sea, a new flower on Robitussin. Please, malicious yurt, please, jump as a real mom on nine Darvocets.

As if Ravel rode the underlying stature of ghosts. Syncopation and ichthyosaurus.

A mini apricot turbulence. A sand squid with fire forming young highways when the quays derive themselves from unbalanced medicine mullets. Fried gusts of wind. Passion and eclair, kill doctoral, pit viper ransom. Eating macarons of god, or say, wild pieces of parrots expelled through business park bushes. A can of cancer pontificates and implores and hanging fallopian Jesuit dress.

There, like me, like cacography calming cheetahs.

TRANSLATING ÉLUARD ON KA'ANAPALI BEACH

everyone lives in Taiwan or China
not to exist in the world of memories
presence sponge
there is a two and a three / a dolphin of breath that is federal and
    warped smoking baby
the fear of gazpacho at midnight / the unmentionable outlandish
    ghost dunes
stalks cut in the razor home / red labrador all madness
that's all it is
horror of ten wolves in time in a man in a shimmery pungent tux in
    a gorgeous canoe
my life is stealth glass but it's still mine
image of love unright talking of huge alabaster
talking of the unrefined Camaro in your little putative residuum
in general women try to prove a cause post-wreck
and icy now now financial chains and black crafts in American
    summer fable
you prove by what you give and violently and remove the grand
    from larceny
a little green rip in every M
a screwy nest of dirt
emboldened by the softest pain or name or circular sheet of wet
    whips
and mainly this is so
from Charleston South Carolina to Cubism / all the entrances to the
    palace are locked from within
it's like Vanuatuan wallpaper / and if I cared to break my word
    I would

THE ONEIRIC AS CAUSTIC BUNNY

only casually-in-death do you fly fish do you name yourself Captain
  Areopagus
or Agincourt
the flowery shade of flowers
prurient avalanche
the guy called me a faggot or covert bulimic image
ballistic Shake Shack it all appears so huge not in Valdosta though

you don't want to see what happens to me as I
break stones with the dawn of breasts

I KNOW EVERYTHING

I know the individual the wave the tenebrous scansion of human
   intent
The indigo spoils of Nebraska day and night
I begin with the New Mexico State Penitentiary riot
Whatever catchy name you come up with I'll put you in your place
The world is half squirrel I probably live in a creek
But there are mere moments to this
Are alive
To dramatize the squalor tax and evening shave
My good friends never talk about ideas
Who in certitude believes the room leaves the dark jumps out at you
   when you run up on the beach
The black openings of the plane
I might see the swimming gin of youthful parachutes
The bottoms of softener bottles from which you weep
Yawping up and the like you know tortillas at the end of the world
   this is one lucky co-star of mine
No no no in Europe the American balloons
In goat trees the shine is a shoe-horn in Russia like humiliation in
   the terra cotta vacuum
Murderous daisy river Saint Laurent like a shoebill in Rwanda
I've seen your liver the stupidest thing ever
I almost said your umbra is rooted in Freemasonry
In this fact lies something that one has no choice but to live one's life
Even in death
In 2010 I learned what a random signature and out of that random
   signature I came to my name
What a villainous salt strain

Tap the loaded messenger as she heats her arrows to a bluish
    empathy
Upon which moment caverns discuss themselves their nautical
    charts exploding into grayscale auroras
Night charts its silver on the pool tables of darker experience
Like a bonus of terror
I hope my mind is fried beyond a barbershop
Walking lotus
What do they do actually unlock the dirty the super ache
I see supreme sexy sex all day for no reason
Their fear of us is the image of us
My dust riddle my lost wave in the desert of deserts
Eyes closed it mattered in the most graphic and balanced of ways it
    mattered in the claim of the curve
Of the wave in the voyeur's house
It spoke like an idiot advisor or a specialist of dream modalities
In sum it asked if there was any connection to this guy this grey guy
Each new day more alive than the distant memories of how the
    poet's spring extends
From my skin to my chief pants
Asleep in you who are people who want to think like the silence of
    the green-dark duck
So you will get up and try on extraterrestrial chaos ocelli without hope
In the silence of the green-dark duck

THE NEW DESNOS

Deep   Deep Verbal grab; & 44 grabs–
listen "(/!$ - Czar"
Throwback from little facsimiles
Gaol way
Maybe give gifts.   Water wine.   Unforgiving zephyrs on.
   Amanuensis question Axiom
My common Quetzalcoatl

I FEEL JUDAS TODAY

New York City / red butchery float
Alas New Mexico / you mean you want bodies
In the slums / a thousand dark chevrons
In the blue wheat of alas
This is the world-green cycle
What did I hear you say the poplars were no good
Did I hear you say reading within is medicine
World-green sky personifies alchemically
But the times don't change / but the orange dragons of them do
Until no one no longer then never to be like this again
Dark arts her mural her basic body
Why am I digging your scene again unsexy woman
I see the messages on angelic fax paper
In a weird Floridian pie chart singularity / save me
This is what they've said about my pataphysical wing
A cosmic fire from your eye is sent
When I see what people do the waves they perform
Outside of their mothers it is something new
A light for other hours / ingesting pork a lot
A harbor of viscous shit
Islands implying foreign felt cops
Hell stays with you as a quiet mental aquarium
Tilted by enough cash to bring about the baby
Give me the jazz in these corals in the vice of the future
I'll be glad when the corpses are sunny side up

GOD WAVE

the wave as veil & veil of wave & you breathe like any dusk can
be harassed poured perused by wild looks the serpent of peace the
oligarchical symbols that murder you in the face of perfection &
the sun was the spoon of sentient rancor prestidigitation & blurring
aquatic oblivion at all times the impregnated complexity of non-night
there exists the rum of spectral avenues so hallucinatory I held
the owl tower the floral pattern from hell in my sight & to think
I could have lost that amphibious glare as I remember its automatic
crepuscular & alien force itself as hierology clemency fervor guattarian
disappearance as biochemical warfare ablative inactual as a phantom
furthering nausea a series of detonations necessary & retinal that
my name is killingly also called concocting the unaverage nascence
feeling the binary vatic of the mouth fabric I said to lord byron the
poet of evening is already between us who feeds our hearts compassion
seasons for several lies for wind fucked ways of emotion pretending
to appear near who let the sexual diminish this absolute zero type
of compulsory guesswork this mortifying reproduction of prose
appropriates to mean electrical in origin or saying goodbye with
the lips of a child to embalm strangers with irregular intimacies
to deprive oneself of detritus involuntarily severing the haphazard
task of our dark & I am also some slow incurable laugh that inimical
wall erected in all sapient places like the cause of hair the cause of
forever's rivers & love is like loving the dream spray of these blood
hieroglyphics & you have eyes that must return to you like one hell of
a wind or I am that laborious maze of minimal presence usual quietude
a lotion of virulent nothings or mauve tulips thoughts of january's
ambulance remaining dressed as bachelor underwater a starburst of
dictation of scars once my love was painting perfect liar to liar I heard

a terrestrial wing like a wall of cops who keep their corporeality all whims I had these lengthy open confusions about causing lush macabre in which case a wave of prescience in the veins only to have ability with hours to waken the pleasurable with idealess symptomatic grandiloquence that I am a hallway of broken facets of the world's world to pass up what calm is coming through you not all star weariness or pythonic infancy not my love again not the singular nuance of repetitious misanthropy those who writhe ventriloquists in the if matter at last forgotten we don't would horses more like the warrior dream the whalebone aesthetic prowling selectively in the letter n a sequence out of air offering the moonish others horrendous kinetics seeing mirrors interspersed where one saw shattering venereal dawn between us you could see other pleasures where their air in flames would be poems & should face that just a miracle would be jail & what people need is a world of what people what loathing what ocean what toy coffins in the toy earth what a staying face as the room had a room none could adore or despise when I was in it that's the earlier thing to say the capital thing overlapping & I cried & was ashamed that death solidifies with imaginary kids with its hand over my other mouth I moved the documents around building relationships with verbal animals whose openness is like the sentimental bombing of sentimental babies in the hot paradise of time & consumption like giving gems to a living gem nothing in the slow sad or perfect very much world but our neurosis is at once to strike the softest blows of non-intention there to slow enigmas of god replication so what is real is what to you & on & on & there are often successions of doubletalk planetary & ceremonious doubly flowered drawing into their praxis obscene motives reproducing flagrant prolonged desire this world does not cease to foreignly call a glimmer or shadow pissing out the human moment is why we grit & out of a new uncanny care things begin to be apocalypse as a way between the whiteness of seething firsts from the skin of fire to no ordinary absence no it costs what it costs audacity suddenly spiraling into confusion & serious firs afloat in olympia forever there is something this drink of shine occludes the wary truth word kindly insisting on ascent & descent to position a fragment showing you putative to have gained all of us convenience no trees a couple of prostitutes to melt in every change of song took off all my rings I could not see but woke to know around accumulations of you & you of not being what worries me genuineness agape in the place of the joke where the children's court is the month of june nauseating replication nauseating logic what cognition must the skin trap able to swim to host float & historicize bodies beginning a perennial act of such nectar drop heat in some irreal fulcrum of space between this idea & symptoms of the ideal forbids another writer to create without ground growing on feeling & apprehension the fourth flowering of art complexion completion I felt money would make amends apropos I know what you think it's right here the weakness to say to you it seems sorry to love you to be original to propel the discontinuous design of the present into this what is not valued worthy referenced aggrandized inspired completely human & from the torqued heart everybody's garbage pursuing pathos she had eyes like desnos justice for the unique the ruins the mental tapes causation stars & must be assigned for data & further as carotid blood sinks & swims in my desolate initials I made money off shit like tyrannical fixation this would be the faintest concealment of blue that hurt the desert & hurt my long lashes these segments of notion aswirl a swan this language of carnivore revelatory double of this age replete with makeable worship in the halves of childhood soft sponge magnetic dream root full of flowers & never achieved then after this played with mineral drowsy fawns riddles about nothing in noting that appearance to stand emergent among standards to live through the infiltration of women scintillation I have no idea how lust exceeds hours in the head rivering a gesture & against eternity tiny articulations real atrophy real rabbits & what they said was merely out of kind of making resentment used to talk to later a friend will call friends & why as an external you is rather simplify our house laying vexatious predicates in the faded cellar hardly what's our avenue but ability habitat mental assignation our faceless cabinet father of the happening reticence out of controversy of is of is of & no other can arrest itself this camera language this is of itself an asterisk moving bodies to finish a margin of error is merely humanistic this signals books in the grammar bible who diseases or maybes in what water colored taoist dry moon dormant entropy in later elevations of this marks upon the cadaverous dusk this feeling was human they said the tears in green

55

how they sang in every color shined in grandmother filled her head
with milk & we were there the wolves this would pool into all the
hopeless ease of mind the last emission to emulate a classical holding
rumor hardly umbrella hardly femur hardly vein clouded blood
where fondness drops ponds lead by you know is all I'm asking for
money not always escalation manure of progress I began thinking the
luxuries to eliminate would be the worst crime or regrettable pyramid
speak we were talking about that word & I don't know what but I
was calling you los angeles confirming a presence I can't clearly of
multifarious rarely need to adjust the damaging to be invited I refute
the shoulds of pupils whose are lucrative barely in the retrospective
polarity mind which means that all is aghast at its imagery mirrors or
should be defense as one day's thoughts settle a rupturing double to
hunger & become the night something yours & involuntary for future
ramification I put on saturday walked outside with pianos talking or
something what you'd call acting out the voluptuous indexical she's
lying in a paper field as if reevaluating blood were enough to make
regarding yourself a blaming I love the double mode of the clock when
it says my love isn't theater but a comet & not a career a ripped susan or
canyon of names a machinated dockside & something's edible to that
effect but in any shape is a coming whose thoughts we think which
chance reflects on its first supposition or what is good or good without
the if phantom of monday avarice when the world calibrates acuity
pardoning me accuracy I believe this ingenuity is a ruse a mouthless
desiccation whose feeling marked the end of an apocalypse poor
dream ascension to hunger then then when the real place is hands in
the sink we can laugh or not place emphasis or ekphrastic but to stir &
wonder about which work hell will better have never does anyway so
my subject becomes what will always profess best to believe intention
without holding on to a governing principle where is the cartesian or
does the winding acknowledge a familial pilfering in the heart of a
mammalian liminal feat whatever it is that guards the head this drink
can have a drink at the well of you casual myth can have can have
me I think if love itself of if objects & put those in justified letter to
make an end or such nonsense whose twin thrives without vanity like
thievery in the mustering over then in the brute hours of chameleon
of course nuclear virgin apocryphal land of the next metonymy &

catacomb of the august novemberness in the paint thinner or wind or small epitaph perfect friend talking serenely & waking the light one couldn't look to take to eye the reality of that or hour or fourth of that or world or would you & was a chemical fixation what they may or may not be or else money is money especially these days sweet rain disturbing index & plundering the kid for deeper song than possible all while wading in what one couldn't fix between the taming of three people three meridian people & I couldn't claim a number as mistake of its form or forms its autoclave or crypt what the salient bath mouth has in store for most crystal stalk of time fabric sore viridian love like night sweats loveseats white night washes her blood doesn't run & her bruise won't leave the evenness of marx the world gives zoologically or blaringly absent from the birth ritual or say life was not handed some directional fire as promethazine escapes itself & osmotically the unknown anima mundi unlike anal sex I say the shore of building nothing was a gift neon should be implicitly crying with infernal horoscope like so many little marjorie perloffs do an idea of banking mental routines sanguinity chestnut color of hair on a particular memory day was fun for talking or kissing in the glow of christian trees where I let my hands fall up & curl through imbalance or to see these slang things not to let the smaller inconsistencies break but her way I have no luck on the same stillness we waved for our hands held sure but what could stop the age from cutting before our smiles rained that route away it becomes like this thrush on the edge of knowing something lustful isn't really it's a frightened sort of keystone by lack of sense or reminiscence but that might be reductive in longer terms of drear how dare I describe an illustration of the otherworldly fucked in the prison of kemetic recollections her falling falls in the other scenes gains speed while talking all the while & leaving or gaining seasons & days & not for the sand the reasons we compare situations like scorekeeping but that marks the eyes intruding upon our holy integral thorough education of lack of heart by not knowing anything is cause for animation again with the colors hers were brown but also dark green in the pink evening louche but not yet that young or maybe just born on radar & many can't praise from there you need to enter a week when the retaken wind excuses you tripling of subjective anonymous continuing tom-toms it's hard on themselves to encourage satiation only orchestras will save now or water but the athletic daylight has no more earring glimmer than a handful or gesture of madness in the cloaked finitude one could call sublime swaddling the artifice closures out of an edenic date making substitutes mother again in the natural fallacy that can verily excuse going from democratic to question from june space to slowing down of the xerox golondrina of redolent parisian pills nothing is wetter than existence luxury opposed to the hands of some air air & in spite of the fact of according to hate in solitude irrational carcass of the sun's flank of air in vagrant air chasing all the lines seizures observations of sophisticated air the shadow of the falcon's bildungsroman my own air without a trace spawn of glissando of watchwords minstrelsy thought garishness from the rarity of eye zoos sever the very thing that power of what should this banking be reaping windows a sort of irreducible but more importantly a major mirror induction non-mechanical muse in what is lurking in light of other things & why anarchical to translate the direness of shifting element into the white threat of empirical order who hunts from the waterfall of the bleak mouth intransigent unfolding of signatures who beads the quiet domes of air with peering at the almost human or childlike answer over anonymous forms parading leering falling clutching from the break of each strand the opening tensing unopening hammering thirsting or desire for the unknowing left & right of natural edges knots in a live spectrum near the crown away from the snowed-in sex the outer rings of the solar plexus whole pupils in the forward going arc-like machine away from the segments taken away from the segments or a mother pushed in for god's sake kingly change the room of the heart the head anthropomorphism in vital oscillations sideways glittering from eyes rise of the sky code for abundant revelation dynamic shifts beneath radiant epiphanic pairs subtle modes for the clanging zeitgeist quota seals splashing rememeberer of time without a positive without an artifice laughter the I meant to be affect imminently verified by shamming a derailed darkness under occidentalism this is all about nothing & then departs this vocal mincing like a watch spring's spring the regular tender nocturnal who says its cage its skin is a wondered spectral what could strum the philosophical static removes their loans to cosmic dearth I have been known to strike out at third things have been called a unique looking thing or at least a knowable artifact in the gutless chain the last allele it felt was immortal coast unjust colors throughout the hex untwinned idea of spiritual detail a gross of flames or harbors not animal day falling pellucid echoer who rouses the eating sun & finds a panacea of herkimers adults & nothing but singulars a flowing hears without one survival survives so little & far above biology absence of placement where the coercive zero should be or have a proper route to dissident other epiphanies other species being our language only not the object of a non-discoverable world or extermination apparatus project a whatever they immerse one hand in water they are not adapting they are also practically nothing spiraling no more than primal love of certainly close blue as an institute of its own but rhizomes are real & the golden whip nest blazing in the stream of enigmas is the same as it was a word is the serious maze of its own disease or what thought could interrupt a scarce escape from bioluminescent hazards a usual dereliction advocating futility vortex a figure-eight servility to star chance or kerosene of the imaginative cathedral dome utterance of the veil I've lost other days wondering adjustments of rain from tender skies over tender corvus over trepidation it's the master saying penumbra's weak larks embers intricacies lobotomy as if to say the beauty of very or verily was mistaken for evil memory determining a fulgent instruction equinoctial photonic philandering for the sequence the thirst for power or polar extreme is thesis incognito earth punching delicacy into hemlock the droves awaiting monstrous forces to dearly uncle uttering the blood is mixed in the carbon wedding one shoe in the basque region one shoe in a mosque in a mosque the earth twinned the ebbing out goes lighted quenching a heightened furtherness dither white in every laceration that is white a third morning or seventh affluent parade envelopment & lungs who said says or page locked-in adherence most of my life is double exposure bursting the real teens sighing in a wasted random coterie roving our estate don't do this to me baby said the earthen mass computational cardiac september but this is still not loneliness the next of the avenue of the stars retreat of guardian fireworks our heart masks a wager a cluster of carnal bourgeois catastrophes that tellurian no longer same a formal artistry the gnomic fouling of two trance voices saussurean these canvases in tormentable increase hidden addictions in a white rose soon in a grey one in a gray one a raven whole & liquored beyond am that lunar bowl of rising through several risible suns resting is all blood washed by the blood glow of the uncanny unseen money freed from itself if friends make their way to more convenient sugar or manifest quicklime in the feminine aqua landscape of distrust also quicklime in the feminine super candelabra of tender exclusion quicklime in the feminine aztec permission from her general first on camera she liked one thing how conscience looked like us boys pretty eyelashes waving away brazil like lost father alternation a story of très heart the same storm blank of theatre safety equals the moon & a big coke once again traversing the factual resentment of not having her as empty light like ending itch sacrilege brewing in this pluperfect sensorium we'll find a palace to ether to all the original flowers hyporeal stimulation down the downtrodden longness of it all if all decimation a kiosk of night or facsimilar maternal system a misnomer for plebeian breaking would note the same pink sheen of rarely unified epistemological quotients surveillance precise the xylophonic touch of intentional gambling the blank blinking before itself & its mode intoning the flesh of our haphazard orchids left to the light's gestation say the devil is in vogue blowing over young fields of other inclination that was the way they did it then electric cadence silvering vertically against any old selenite mercy cleaving these houses from the hurt of fin de siècle lost his love remains his love skills itself in dearing the rooted the road his eyes & on her less in its black cube a future inextricability of wristwatches of multiple salacious sets of tears or human solitudes oneiric goodbyes out of everness rhomboid ulterior malady the ocean squares equate to hang-ups in some episodic about what we could say before ordinary swallow of swallows to want one's exegesis supernumerary lucid envelopes of writing wisps of hair for tiny often intersections discovering the grass of lincoln park for the first time the inescapability of a culture continent of gold standard concealing time to purify when the only reminiscent urinal baseball game in cold blood cheers the political synthetic rose & hermetically in her head like rose pure light could occur the brilliance of readymade lines I loved putting myself in the raw of the neighborhood curating a viscous reality of wanting subjects of what or thereness the temporary germaneness of lust awakens possession of that ardor the movie said the avant-garde restoration program or otherworldly estragonism or hubris or the height of regular squirrels on a telephonic periphery meaning a glossy sutra a value suspenseful the fragmented admirable dissident genera this species of oak in cohesion mantras denials of laughter instantiate a mortal lyceum of compassion enigmas my friend & only real himself on dynamic banks of removal desire as an act as the debut of deadpan three sobs the either level talisman with the essence very supportive to rendezvous some who never sanguine paradise moved to a gorgeous vacation echelon the incandescent no one's excavation in the sea the escaped capital almost died instantly under the notion that movement is superb in itself the inward stare involving conscious alibis hostages coalescing into certain correlated selves I thought contained the urban several acquiescing & flooding star street can't undo without a single duty toward the labyrinth to have futures before one knew loss before one knew loss one became the endless emergency of past emotion our aughts adamant with forms of sublimation predetermined ring & shimmer holograph hotel is the day of clear hunger draft of morning emptily gesturing at a friend's laughter which is milk beautifully built seeking endlessness then in the physical new orleans michael keenan to discover mirrors a sleek look & there will discover the remembering gift was at hand to insure you should not have been alone that day you did you could not reach the functional the source it's funny the growing in certain parts of the cities anyway there are grounds grounds at times to allow mantic faces to present in the face of it an absolute ossifying result that logically tells stories finally to learn the worst for she goes to sever a dream received there to dissatisfy the deaf combination of attitudes with chronic if your inventiveness is the insane & aimless profanity of futures we are here beyond themselves as vision as the magic summation of day fades the new new set of stars gauging documents of a language cold in the last glimpse of everything a scene of absolute america itself in its own language of languages lowering the subject into a rest of diamond dark gone & never upon anything but the space thereafter the space of sound that even in silence is blank sight the syncopated of matrimony & arsenal the residue hard blue understanding the unbound lecture hearts sophisticated like a lasting lowering fierce source of tender has been a supplication a death code & what is the difference weakened behind her method laconic beauty in asymptote combined with know-how liberation to an arbitrary onlooker to inspire mechanical lunar poems the hourglass intention to inhabit us uxorious the arms dealing inquiry a requisite delicacy moreover the tongue has reaped a leopard print of fashionable fear superfluous rome & then or was it sakakah hermosillo unction alongside process follows a going away night phase forking lowly among the mothered bulletins again the substance was spain he our coast of delicate power our words not solid in the ceasing emotion the sitting room required marquis de sade to learn ditto & say smaller children in our minds I who hang wildly between the etiquettes of coolly satisfied histories on par with loner reality & mutation & winter on the mind living among minor catachresis hubristic battery dissociative symbolist moniker the natural order of sharp objects in the rest the foundation of a migrant sound in the rest a sacred licorice in the rest the stirring american ice & in the rest the hanged man's hands in the night he couldn't stand the unalterable following that it has some if not all or for plant life to be specific is what he said as if the species were important that tiny logical image beginning with josephine avowal of kinetic sorts of presence to further the discourse of original energy by means of diction & original energy somehow told her that her age would come to the very cordial voice of a situation she marred the saturnine spring voyage creature conceding to the unstable paragon rainbow in important books the world of copying the world shadow value & everything I believed in began to purify to the point of war making tomorrow either estimation or forward but static edge eloping you hope you won't devolve to I titled it extremities under heaven & out of libidinous intuition sold its serpentiform maps the radical service of the flower is now the seething dementia under glass is now medium orange trees to make a word appear to make a solid past of the carolingian mansion only guessing at the sporadic what camouflage of love to live on the quiet & summered planet of stars & hell babies acute upon the dust of such a world metal grease & skin ice & apocalypse a serious maze & new is only for what you sell yourself addiction to everything everything betrothed to ocean a guess of collaborative bodies & don't magic of our fascination gulf daily who to reduce who to kill the precise occultation even is a dear fraud heartache a democracy & popular between the real & the newborn networks of eyesight coinciding nights or rapture of memory is he is & what makes the grey figure of himself so uncompromising holding on to cascades is what originality again a holding on parade is wet or aboriginal anywhere to be in a known sense a gentleman said on the matter of depleted uranium all is signed in the hemispheres of police & pop having had enough of the predetermination styles he reaches an ex-pulsation doubtless my harm does awayness so I leave these to one to draw out inaction for instance the sinful ocean as application for the newer oh my grandfather at the senses & go ahead & die & come back aqueous then say the same things repeatedly so gravity or discontent incriminating from back when but then I guess the christ thing coming through pigeons a way back & agon of coincidence the looked-in ahead of time with one right & one left the great examining scene it so happens the actual description hasn't even around you & settlement is taken to apart from hover we've lived through cash opposition & target atrocities this is just a curated fortune & series of singles in exotic wind fusing deathly rolling lots against the commoners no pretense of ghost can say programmatic while outside the voice demeans winds increase of dynasty severed at the point of insignificant demeanor at last to fool a moral program unused reprisal fiction & that was what his description held plain in the evaporation of worlds & I wish I could write like that like him in those monotonous halls of elucidation it was a world & that was invigorating inviting the fragment party where everyone had an ebbing slowly had a flush meditation with all the ruthless wanted & moved with race in money which are equals & forces of great eclipse to margin with that foolish light or light another portraiture of a hundred days blowing by or surely terrific seals of blood suiting loosely savored meanings come to acknowledge our subject to hotly educate in pattern the drive the moment every moment is thought coming concerned under itself would process & I think I am another one thing leading to feeling only on only catalyst of the rhizome dation wasn't occipital & yet somehow a breath a barrenness splayed by events had sold itself rhythm fretwork & departure the right-handed there where some

time remained in prose to cry cashmere into skeleton motto heaving
buddhist waterfall bloodlines about the carcass & chessboard & I'm
picking him up on sunset the hottest day on earth was still on earth
they used reason to abstract & abstraction to reason irreal catechism
the lineated abstract or incombustible the abstract sword of clarity the
thomas pynchon the engagement of threes in 13 days in 13 boxes days
in the mirrored box the dead accomplish thereness it was sad that one
letter ended the cessation drug halved should one right & been only
in one the educational fluid flowers or manikins their pain was all
one lifelike tour intermodal nude accentuation capricorn of falling
water reminiscent urge jumping rock to rock & pagination of rock
metamorphosed fragrance accidents happen within species only or
not only but wholly the decorative is not is not the promenading
spring it is called devourer fallacious dove clear drive the suite of
clinical ice cream in summary hundreds of miscarriages their deaf
telling dream coats about us what of this offense to write about
the last ragged ray the heart-shaped sofa gulags of wind passengers
as lovers demented with each blush or following the arcs of crazy
accruing smoke alone or recollected as in afraid of other people's
demands the other poets love against anything measured like that
blood in the emerald socket from me to you the wow & ha & local
anathema or the way it was when through & through a dive toward
solemn gristle the burning author herself the resounding door lock
looking out of bounds heaving elevators from the dead's reach
dreamstate's focus manner & fulgent nova remember back with the
okay clarions or the willful lantern embodies the veranda adroit
didactic hubristic fruit basket of fluency oh eros the powered the
pill-popping molecular in eye art that gradual heist in which he holds
his breath like some ramshackle sundown is clear entropy atomic
indelible as rimbaud's potion the white akashic boundaries the jail
white discussion of novae lover tracing the hex in ellipsis the lasting
remark whitely tracing the fog of fuck the fragrance of smoke the
finger in the ink in the pussy the law of the desert the waves all
shadowed the smile of god snorting coke in pussy hotels the pussy
in the cock the windows of the clit to fuck in blood in the boots of
the heart the hard heart the dead & their dead fear of gods' cocks
my balls in the mouth of the earth this machine kills shadows arcane

fires unmoved obelisks instruments free music from the symbols
& throwing their heads back laughing unknowing a vagueness
chromatic as this is moral contraption asleep in the eyes for lighter
light substitutes fortunate for disgust that saturdays estimate on zero
days the blood of the storefront the stork as cinema unto that fading
away in the driven looking star duct of dining desires are something
in the medical petals of surrender while the music played he worked
by dandelion green his unction in the trappist process here's the
beauty part too removing hair & diamonds from the foam a laser
should or veiled sea the body was a tipping point ode of example
to human from mud & all other contagions along a lasting burner
eternity is correct the sign of changing light is what we own a
mathematical number the precepts are true as precepts nothing truer
only better são paulo & ether tonight but we could go away from
here I wish & I seethe in the mortal idea tree breaths that was worth
a powder blue emotion like spontaneous blue should what transform
from loneliness oh having done what got one photogenic ecstasy
motherfucker reaped in the densest night a favor for action in the
kind views against a comma as lecture or reportage or games made
of acceptable camaraderie to adjust to a savior in hallways of sound
floating last like happiness any thing was collapsible light put upon
the one with the other as telephonic cross message unmanning our
wings escalating in the death house to phantom shower where no one
can see the prying side or come close our privy unsympathetic to
& a famous necromantic why loose universal picking things off the
longshot lawn seeing blank children in a demonic difference wit the
quit to come closer said who knows & why couldn't a man answer
the father in the father's faith a thousand years or more pulling into
the sun & the subject of hope to have some acting out on cassette
feasible in fevers suited to a definitive victim who is put to sleep holds
on to to fire keeps painfully of restorative flow alkaline pith of time
absconds with our fall through grains of star the delicate skin washes
the sea of a darkness that couldn't halve its prescriptions court date
of flowering deadline her staccato innocence or to fool to share the
moon the testament in rows of fruit of the systematic family what
he said was haunted the head honest in thoroughness & stooped in
its place of heaven on ice & that was the only word in keeping with

the picture hazards to hundreds of lives was trying to preach to fly to inchoate semblance murder is murder murder is chosen order is human the cage of the floor is murder as said to tell the fluctuations I knew that too late is offered by the skull of orphaned breathing slowly the seconds come to raise an animal firmament an animal was it came to be the raw of the eye keep staving off radiation or radiation however note the theme was wasting something this night but long is not the dread to strip down after left yearlong flows the passionate sort to encompass a mask sporting the verdant gestural flood the capital to change the changes inoperative & lauded by the very verb the horoscope had its march enough chartreuse returns our slogans & stripping desperate inverted carbon within earshot & stride though it knew to say no though it knew to be a blanket alive faraway tribute shards of crazy in profile the evening of sartor resartus the one rising to through walls of lightning & snow fortune as the carthage of night with weapons of celebration reviewed anew added some touching game to obscurity local worth cardiac event puerile detachment from the life of space they paid her a sort of jasmine astride dishonest logos jupiter to cheat hanging fruit by locus gypsum germane & cloy credit in the years to come they wived a friend they loafed in the enchantments of dimension handled like pink dew the dew our guts of fever utilized the sloughs of deafening artifacts fustian sand blank rose the phone began to body & though we leave though our money loved the yucatan comforts it starred itself on delayed weather slots on the starred famous on earth & not-earth when I align myself in art categorically existence love bringing one thing to the table audibly apropos of human error child erasure sovereign point of the athletic lyric the white women on the beach of the broken consortium deaf seal carcass last scent from the rocks waking ocean & wet light on sacred envelope a quasar unforgiving & throwing down the heirs while enumerating & novelizing deaths attitude is not a game is serious with beauty in the backlashed number intimation inundated photographic disgust poignant to stop & had a penchant chanting for hurt in our indecision & ignorance of names ark of the choice & the while in the house the hundreds of percentile women in their passionates lost luster & fabric of time down & breathing meat a pale tree & custodial maneuver was prettier than anyone expected

& starker too but she climbed so soon in my image sided with his his
ok evil his eager littoral her focus was a catching thud under rounds
of nature but she can't fight the green room he puts in his pocket &
keeping time in a water's collapse weakened his love was different
than hers especially on the tea saucer in the catacomb & floral her
acres of lenses puts a cotton wolf through his windshield for poverty
she reaches for the bell eschewing the blue meat of something produc-
tively said wasted on hearthside omnipotence glint of looking out at
locked geometry became the boyish hobby of my country in straight
volume in closed elocution the empty pharmakon or loose registers
of monday evening dreams on causation titular & saintly tethered
relaying their drills with tender decay half venture deviant fragrance
of neurotic supporters & baby images fairer the black & white looker
fairer the idea in wordgames a tongue unhinged from its estimates
the having of one's own friends is a farce a normal flare or glamorous
exsanguination housing go insane to remember the better was
beaten once the pieces fell better under guidance growing weather
its youth in the precipitant future diffusive sequencing thing & take
for spreading love until the end of wandering damage we become
weeds become & to find a way through symbols one battles through
selves through night become the night in another way in the eruption
of night the aesthetic impression a lonely insignificance in denim &
speaking childishly sequence of blood its emotional soul black in the
scene for dollars or of course avoidance resentment dilating her life
going to decadence in a momentous pacific moral excitation that
is renown gladly as generosity willing what had been done to lose
cloud walks & the likeness of a torch to the mind the mind in its skull
pulling the vagrant frictional number once more & once more when
I will marry also grave for a buoyant native fog or set on love & hate
mode the ulterior sound a thousand plateaus for winter gone don't ask
of our rebellion godly pursuing mother's hair with inaugural inferno
references to cornmeal to mammalian teeth & occasional purity I was
a god walker in some cocteau film gun-battle in milk iron paradise
melanin of au revoir to skylight mercy & warm succor female mask
urgent source of necklace to where manikins palomas beautiful
futures is toward the shore tending to depth astragalus of inclement
depth on the veritable the structure of their hive in plain view of

mutual facts then looks were all gifts from the same dawn settling dimension egregious in contract the greenest eye was geometry in the hallways of the hallways of molecular facsimile & no human qualities darling but those of a singular affect live as ecstatic mineral in empty figure inclined to static or small parts of gruel & rhyme blood with photogenic flags in the universal shatter & king the autumnal bluish urges bluing sentiment typically reserved for imperial the poet sees cadence in a threshing white diffraction of afternoon suns artist of meteor & ashen spilling mandarin the order of something much more than primal gestures annulled in the cardiac sprigs of marriage a dive to night & audio helium bathhouse kid amid apparent coagulations variables as de facto engineering trophy of unison as accent critiqued by oasis ruinous quintessential doctrine sacred inundation where one holds death on a bed of death the last occasion lavender paraplegia all a game to the unaffiliated outlasting lives on the planet video kingdom disfigured amateur matter in regard to relationships rolling iodine the body a shadow ship in general drunkenness or just a horrific animal among the churches honorable waking urgent foaming in the masterful all this thing this thing arcades of safe posture fingers of the mind the he in he takes dementia actual or common a broken throat undeserved style distracted women over all a hundred grand poolside splash the dreams they get from your queer womb something like that daimon or new wave to determine the severed soaring kind of coin the trains of an electric clime he remembered one thing solitude in the scathing connecticut brevity loitering in a field of veritable complex our faith knew less than you shouldered the courageous lie glassless about the wavering street enigmas like killing used to divine antics or smolder fruit to the touch the white gloves present to the ken of glowing fountains our mouths our chestnut shootouts she likes him for something phoenician to play the part or live the part does the business reach the status of what I'm cutting real smooth the generators in your methamphetamine brotherhood you want to be making moves on the street there is no dialectic standard what the fuck I need to get done this burden to be so memorific detrimental why I'm here the reading material involved in homicide gets calls all the time gets calls all the time is I don't care & saw that about me fucked up is the beginning inverted translucent backwards &

forwards is sublimation rowling around all night stretching this guy under the names dashes the names lines with red in the dark nor a dress she likes the way he acts especially when he can't like that is what every metropolis a sacrifice for catabasis profit by shimmer by marvel casualty by grey by only sold for micturition obstacles pouring from the face & there is none the so-called focal phantoms stepping up their bachelor caskets calling out blood to bluff with weighted branch the cascading shapes without pre-determined cash unchanging redress the differential living water the breath was always there it says that there has been & watching one sleep occurs as the past of synchronic posing rooms overdose of situation in the mild differentiation of self a bottomless grace fire & stars are shown like seafloor seraphim the false bone plane learning of service over ruthless habitation emulation series of whirling babies forcing those things to happen speak orchestration orchestrating a tortuous incision of the dance it could be said it could be said on a saturday on earth in beijing grazing with the features you know so well the editorial cosmos there heaving a new place toward sleep watching us stance the part where the wind creeps in the room & wakes you with its fuckery is it the permanent delivery of harebrained the peeking the mantra conduction odium & medication & the process it undergoes to become such & leave such & such out for once the sanguine could not speak office of my heart neutral corridor collapsing & their suicides with quelling of every animal holding then labeled deceased or at least quite a manipulation enigmatic mile orange catalogue of man hours not to remark with omens above genesis we have black brown white as pure electron in sigils of nouveau needing an image & a scene to write when one is not in the forest & say we are doomed cinematic lux of going indifferent is one life the other is a good assortment of momentums the pious doubting house exits blueprints of double vision near parallax but it was the evening consumption over centuries that can succumb to honor you have a choice without a ship without a choice itself in romanticism inference & a city of computer creaming inane fight of water & the new creatures or dreams in expectation of blue to see your child tearing the root of weather's roots infallible & significant tuxedo posture as has in mind & to assume the mind is a machine or facet of referenced group came surly to pronounce its name in cadres the like last academy was having room introduced to codify the ghost in all the pieces happenings of front doors vegetal burnings of lascivious summer bridges to indict the verity of anything in my mind in the casino business in the looking through said architecture with emptiness infection desire to know what vacuum absence or space will animate immovable virtues a length of fear a seeming lucid querying born the wrong kind of filmmaker losing an ill word to phosphorous drastic no parentage cannot stop the dilution superabundance accrual of private sectors the the vocal light salvages our indecent yes questions records of refugee motion animated kind & now the sky but real & total lottery stakes to pray like hawaiian punch oceanic bye tone engulfment too to be a hand seems luckier in theory's mirror bed rectilinear figures swooping manikins with which to troll the sea like & liking the recreated the sinister genus fondle I only like to look bare taught reframed though so influx to a nest that casually I gain pluralistic handicaps icicles or code-reds dice capital sleepily seducing war for general then something remarkable a secret defeated in seeing without knowing white as surgery resuscitating every nanosecond for the sake of the image of orange oration like fool for the fire's infant as if causes or catacombs in freelance derivation or precluding what was heard in senior damage was our symphonies & substantial asking we gathered doves for the marathon dress astride their operations & skilled floors of attention the kind that could the kind of avenue to reimburse the sea's discontent simple aspirant likable scars of the flag human from depiction here is your pattern in the future becoming huge cornfields where totems cancel one quiet lark or protozoan confidence this fulfillment the said candy in parliamentary to want a language for nothing with our half of the good looks complete dislocation in doing hundreds of travesties in front of people then actual people & that was sad with music dislodging night between my air & your floor thousands of waterfall fugues weapons wings or worlds of opinion & you get the picture whatever & the phone law the new disgust or threading this & that with xanax & y z being the -ing starving sudden children devoured above an ultraviolet beach these said things already here where I should be along doing fringe routines for their exes wads of cash become asseveration persuaded whose in & leisurely out

70

& of the apartment became someone smaller than tin such were confessions experiments of the unfelt what becomes real in this ear later on was a lost dialogical a seagull monitor to a space unlocked from out the air was a door at most inconsistency floundering romanian colors to verge palm fronds escaping from the inside the numinous emblazoned by the captain of the open forum turning solemn went by & we had it all the choices of formality & relocating leos on one hand cameras playing & then wringing out a tree of breath absence where once knew other bodies off limits like tainting nothing but transcription or what could be the company's footnotes forgetting echo park a slowly gathering coming greenly spilling etcetera two returns opined blankly & repetitious surrounding a patriarch who chances wide unremedied delusion paper airfare the able red & black of all you don't need opening knower having sensation to fear heeding a thread as everything said has something to do with everything said like bread to indeterminants amalgamation of every real counterpart for does he does the red book exist do the draughts enable us for coming seclusion its parts to be the it's amicable the way to lovers for what in the ebbing house of profile & belong or the reason for emblem solid parade for an appetite cluster as morning blood dumps the annual night & one's mind has a place for dominoes for touching weathervanes to talk to gather one's life rope in lengths of semantic squealing that one is being talked down being cradled in some existence from which it never escapes says what one should not listening to force to relive some idea of the fiery clean that deplores us & sends our bodies to an in-between sex or just vetiver fascist state of writhing in the right room & foolish infinite we cannot blame the we can about which the can part can only fantasize surfing impetuous helium plateaus all purple for denial is too a measured alhambra conduit to another such genius or deuteronomy puzzle such bad backgammon epistolary & smoke sustained a little imaginary omen at one time the bleeding or belonging miracle to attain within one's self-element of faith the pure location of poetries dark marked by reaping sudden prosody oscillations breaths totality says a ripening animal wide-awake detailed in the beautiful blueness there is of catch darlings possessing ideal devouring circles & so the sky's been done before & normative bullshit to grow the fuck up to

71

get to the point the soul's artaud unto purple contusions the beach blankets the malleable contraband artists for the downtown attacks of gold & cocaine this finger used once by one actor & survived decapitation sudden loops & nothing but the designated in a funeral home a demonstration a removal of the inconsistent rain the votive tossed around deconstruction or ghosts protected by intuition asked to become some resident money some handsome lower order vanguard asked once again to make a choice between born alive & yes running if you want running to a detached feeling descartes plain & immobile hounded laughter is like this sometimes in permanent spanish at times the world becomes a power louvre on a list in a phonebook type of surroundable suspense was a love not predictable to come away with pre-determined styles & questions breathing at the limits of any gamble from line devious yet regular & sudden deriving pleasure from my own interlocking motions my evidence succumbing to prophecy some flimflam titular recovery suicide in the margin holy christ or fending off a fax time becomes too much in your periphery & I remember something more about the hotel hand formations the dead carry & carry & the light scent gleaming uncertainty that I was in this case a violet timekeeper resisted the meaning of death at breakfast & other parts of liquid human day deity of surface circulation overprotective of history & numberless epigram anaxagoras said the earth swallows poets of soft & irreducible leisure killing heat & inside the editorial scale of atrophy apolitical dark gorgeous stone tongue a legend of instinctual capital locus cyanide & feasible prop the morning we ate crucified light like bismuth when it enters sisterhood become laboratory for an early prologue reminder western praxis illegal abundance the vocal & abysmal candor he took as casual subtext as one thousand lines of the end plain or configured to deepen the already symbolic lease on season night was corrupted & listening to the clothing listening & to veritas of two aloof where they are they lie in april it did it in the context of it did it it said looking for a biological faraway suffering dogs & you with your children so did the nothing holistically love to reach you will tell you are alone & will tell you that one is not what you are the belief you have chosen police to die for for the exercised deadliest sight was of those places involved you & sight or the sight of both but that's all it could ever seem was done & over with it or later when it all begins to take the shape we see it giving or do we give it the shape it wants in disregard the pride of one hand flashing worth of the other that which not only merits appraisal but also sincere reflection & dialogue loquacious but ever under assignment feeding back you are now no longer there there is clothing on the clothesline you are now no longer there a clothespin on the clothing & arrangement you are now no longer there the city or divine check with the black side of things you are now no longer there before one believes water is seven water is done with such sameness in the sunday luck of los angeles the most eastern city in america you are now no longer there everything elegance good jobs indicators the sky matters at some point before occasionally quixotic registered feeling phenomenon a quiet sort of alcohol that replaces the top emotions diamonds if any cordial throes on the balcony I ruminate & resign lenin himself into the tame of iteration thereof rowing back to a sensational ergo or subspecies of medallions are coming for the dead joining a soft limb with a land of permanence what they say though some sound like speakers inflammatory john cage-style afternoons the breathing of the book when written from stimulation or to be put in artificial order yearning letter & a letter thrown from its double image the inside rejected through shallow minor the engagement & the time as not yours I am sorry & sorrow is inside the etiological domain to reiterate to sever the drawing drawing itself itself the attitude of the passage to the immoral door truism of the fleshy wallpaper felt ruined by repentance of feeling was there in refutation in being some patent suicide to the head or mind or health from you to youth or against theater of you & after adrenaline the stupefactions go or alcoholic by thinking against terminal coloration inclined to here & now the action younger sort of thievish & dreamscape into a nude later in purview the vivid few going onward to illicit crowding cruising dimensions offering & theorized to receive incredible cirrus & coins break funny lexicon androgynous gunslinger of grotesque finesse attractive to any x amount of lucrative long nights along the akin asking in plural babble a problem that hasn't saturated secret holds of shit paintings & shit poems becoming a god becoming torque & complete nullity before any thought is the real meaning of pretense the boom of brain air electronic & was the future of co-existence in sounds beyond a red vision of the same a diamond head & ulterior sorrow a swallow loudly notational conspired to evolve feelings into greater harmonies & they sort of liked it & morning pornography & cigarettes & in showers it had enough of the fondled ring it sorted out fugues of afterlife processes of yesterday day to them & to it it became it & iterated something to swallow the air & sea & earth from inside a well suited for nothing it touched on the scripts of thought without naming it it used without meaning used it blew out the heat of our fears to die in a world with one unnatural ember it lit up the tunnel's vintage & is the perfect image of one according to humility to modes of I am not doing this act cutting as I would like to creatures on some uranium horizon heaping or hearing the pure delusional affect a maker having blown what's going on the possibility of the page of modern dissensions of I know what's been doing been reading going on about codes or desires or detriment a vitamin plain in this fervor called enter where the killing starts to hell with the levees radiant ore to order among beings the very quaint tones the same ones of I'm so oneiric sitting here & there to overcome ambivalent recording stares & there to type of a crematorium every last detail manifests a public state of writtens on tables of generation articles of firework there is a damned thing as 7 & 60 they say the sort of income never ok but we'll never be happy using the casino's candy it's cheaper than whoring out the watching spills of panorama marking until the piano fields wheat in the office of cars & bodies the situation consists of purple bodily intended castle of neuroses in fissure ecstasy of the kingdom of the seal of the kingdom of coming & going to the picaresque sparrow on the iron grate obeying the bleeding future artist decadent sailor of magnesium parisian & earnest forms of film & they walked on curious as things & beings agonizing display of consequence people doing nothing & to fuck in a single note a drawing of what became of women on the other days this thing happened the broken window mattered assonance & delicious persona of southern california wildfires mattered a version of auspicious opportunity & connection mattered to be related in causation to believe in unified results do you miss who you really miss or do they seem as something undone something received as by degrees of each gesture the creativity

& confluence of always breathing & that raving lunar toy in the mist waving despotic vibrations to push something when you are voyaging is another thing than being known like suppose it is easter the gore is missing molested by elegiac cyberspace for the last time verily polaroid the volume to replace chiasmus a minotaur year it's been look I must slave over weapons of holy increase for powder for victims of laughing electively desolate tone proper convictions living theme to change crystalline images there intense beauty shunned completely silence only as stage caught without order lust I have said it furtively a thing could happen along the way a way using the dreams of america in its most painted way monologue appearing not to know the names of cities those cities of all scripture its friend its own friend & passionate who walks away from the accidental idea of them still within still new breaks it has that desire for the word that washing archaeology or regeneration of stab wounds the art itself is only lives to spare for change in the world's they come up to the fountain of democracy with a tourmaline lover to destroy the mania of something breathing here it is here & to the open existence the way to reward florida was duty scientific auras as if the answer to spring has a purpose to combat the frail sandcastles are flowing back spit & the few the hundred reasons for inverting black dress & glare & today I am not bothered by forever its largest sound it begins with something unwondered even with loneliness & poise it so happens that what could not break any bones is heir lover understood by the obsequious searing saliva that has suns & it's as if pioneer subjugating orb & needle subversive repeater the reindeer mansions within this one room intrepid capacity to demand does not look to end catalogue chemistry doing surprising reconnaissance transparent & at certain seaside distance remaining plasticity & conscience we called them combinations keepsakes in expertise volume & their silver wolves are central to extend its play perfectly honed how death of consciousness is thought also & one with irrevocable fragments drawn out the only thing of silent solitaries the way to death by means of work within one's own I do not know the internal constitution of other men or even of thine whom I now address the subtitular epitome of divine relenting the restless list that begins with the makers the claim to electricity genealogy towards what one considers magnified imbalance the thought becomes a thought not the name of thought or the moment of an ethereal wave what is using the still mind still in its creation the still conclusion of thought in stilted speaking states of an atavistic mind nervously to cooperate etcetera mimicry of itself through cervantes to reincarnate something remembering everything it resembled without knowing anything & then it breaks one day & totality all over again process & trace & shadow & all the other parts it has a beginning that becomes every art & its placement in the world of things become art to say money is another concept behind the previous sublime morning paper of a rectangular dwelling symptoms of incomplete attrition the attack on day then night refusal to say the garden the poet is the same sad & withered streak of poison in each green movement the self-contained face of drugs going to speak in a man's place revering eagles of imitation the capable & their ways composure in the smallest car seeming to other people a darker sorter seasonal looming & women opposite the universe blakean monogamy in space time show human ok blooming of geometric years constitutes you you simple binary capital host & guess about the others then nothing in vain I on fire at times believe & disbelieve your logo your need to seethe in crystal flats or masturbating to grieve the human patiently like up next is a weekend of the week your ticketed sun filtering & withdrawn to distinguish what the coming of the luxury of definition the populous harvest of smiles I have come to sleep & destroy the sleeping I own the gun & the slogan sectio aurea bread playing for money & I gamble younglings saying seriously spitting in the urns of gravel the entire seduction of zero & who sings & thinks he is a mortal temperature is not trust abandoning banks calmly the situation the always game energy in the direction of the situation it's like living with paint & panic appearance began as a thursday began as a systematic capacity as energetic summer alerts & that is that as opaque body at full-tilt was parallax waves to worship to feel the nether & say favoritism I will trip should a circus think of possibility of the verge & dreamful commercialism latent spoliation of magic to ossify babies born around the sun your blood goes up & down tomorrow should seek out the world of the sun with utter ambition to season the luck blade our stirring stirs through mammal laboring through sleep through verbs style was

76

girls who turned death's crux into their eggshell original & open with arced events only in major cooperative deeply fortuitous blue as the glass weakened light within the home they kept saying this was up & coming or that that was & is soon to be margins of history like who loves her & stirs to change the boring life she let leave shows the strangled single self anonymously to have fun in the cities of tentative enervation there wasn't a day without gauze whiter gauze evinced at beachside or some confusion eponymous reduction of time in a coordinated response being bergsonian toward the full motion of seething found pinkly being there within arrangements of shadow shadows arranging a wheel of blood or fiction mouth from word evidenced & unwhole an I the purity of money in a faceless basket dinner & disease a word to arrest the average lottery & locus of the year the coeval monuments blacken everything the ear the featured curse of cause a renaissance & the actual moment of numbers incapacitated substance believing the musical rose like coming & making more a sense of noise creeping closer to gods than a god fear arose the autumn arose a fear of her diamond shape in a minute cause of self became a livid fascination for possibly several courage it takes of reviewable life having version & constitution thereof creation in you & creation within to seeable & foreseeable is what I as I would normally confer upon the guests of my life ending universes like fucking ascertainment preconception what do they say to explain & what have I really done besides nothing the purposeful that is not beauty is not explained yet that is also beauty beautiful & there is no world to foreground the absence of intention continues an earlier mentality where moment became order the lesser in a way that combined the world with earth & a point & a meaning show me your your new things complete with parallels & abstract denials of faith the view from here is infamous drama with dissent or unnamable window catastrophe that the seasons infringe continually that what is & what is & what is not & what is not & how does forthcoming breath teleologically massacre not about only through only through & here we have sentience otherwise a signal sentiment to meddle with the average alien with evolution season being the second life of language the era to earn themselves in a smiling caustic immensity to come & engage the senses place names hung from the sun black but these poverties are not real not

concentric effort unnerving end of render to breaking & showing
that has a face called & scaled to her so her imaginary eyes cupped a
belgian sun & thought of being behind that sun human to a degree but
notwithstanding lurid intrusion deserving people in places everyday
I might go blind & the quit comes clearly to describe information
human information to be it snowed of you hand to foot instilled in
me a breathless apperception theoretical milkshake then on the blank
side breath & rent I believed in eating lunch I believed in somatic
ambulance our defeat in real theater sports the game a fantastic reason
to support arrival her sweet threw tired living the knowing moment
when a green world & bothered of blue & gold the friendship portion
was climbing like that unmusical with tilth & tint & answer the
glimmering console most of my dreams dreamed to which the nearest
drugstore came close seduction like spring rays the pain of all that
pushing itself into a total visual skyscraper drawing those dreams we
drive until we imagine some return to top the graphic top in the end
the unfinished & cubic sweet I had the detail of that civic blueness
sort of resentful now which benjamin would call the deference of
oblique communion inside the cop car avidity honestly people throw
meaningless staccato abysmal hieroglyph children dissolving at the
wheel eating meat the things we believe in become our execution
over & over material so great that memory will someday co-pilot it
its value something clear meaning suitable untreasured becoming a
poem the reader sees her plane as the supraconscious real seclusion
of tethering obligatory expectation to data anarchical desirous
felonious prescient entropic severe etymology of undergoing a mouth
monitoring occidental episodics throbbing into poetic ontology of
it they said reasons come with a world of extremes travel due to
undiscovered black & white paradigm in a wayward mile that answers
to the time in memory juvenile windows blowing about ranges of
nearness of such destitute foreign pier some tailored glowing seeming
through the necklaced like night whose appeals in my husband's
holocaust fighting with little tongues of silver & lifelessness I grew
dearly tired of the returns where she could stand popping her
knuckles or understand ametrine from which the lotus slits the throat
a savory precedent a grocery bag full of ideals of sunflower monopoly
the dedicatory jazz music flowing epigrammatically to some blunder

a certain cherry blossom nightmare a human arm breaking on its own planet & the fireplace travels with something under the fire the subsequent jungle puzzle the random punctuations of light their ordinary wedding heresy & coronal muscle mass of enumeration & sex going to go seek a circle & consumption techniques that pit the satanic stars of our frivolous wedding day gloat a disorderly velocity whips a dear word from the notes to scandalize our come & question newborn plumage they have a secret way to tarnish the volume seriously night recedes with blue magical & the seal of annihilation beauties the fruit & verdant horses the red grass of hitman rhythms in a famous ghost benevolence handkerchief in the handkerchief's golden shield & garden to folly wearing neckties with cool patience for affordable revolt a fair fluorescent image in the root names & avoid no spring no sizing up of the skullcap something says entity have locomotion to have a saying & then weaken the future with little keys the seeds in these furrows of monetary virtual seamlessness the decorative marching a something song concurrent with demonstrations of local receipt said segments of a body misconstrue the swaggering look around human apples there will be viable eclipse the ellipse of the channel coming over dawn later names for such phenomenon by theme & suit they had memories of that minute is something that fragments within the whole & exceeds through & obviously cancellation sometimes escalates subsides under birch trees handing down elegant mistakes thrown to the shadow of things that hide in their duplicity I have hands noise to abuse the the place of my birth accept what they have to symbolize their signs some images that have gathered in a modern composite sudden waking without an eye an ornament to delight the sugar of this world violence absolute dance of sun's self-habitat of growth sugar the sudden theme of sugar now a sort of committee spills hectic when I space out & tell pathetic happenings rapacious façade earth as cabinet for june & july a mockery of themes its decorative insignificance the antechamber of destruction & hallucination & houses crisp of light in vastness to contact some image & face the grandmother machine drops new dolls into frozen etiquette appointment of planetary remarks so many commands are made by things to be said about the course of things departure & arrival times movements so close & reclusive most people have found them simple & substituted aim to wait for the world to collide with a vacuous point out there when followings combined believe then in posture time light & in this thing asking for error horror for static emoting anatomically terse & vibrant closure units havoc in a peripheral then then when also forward words indeed performed movements of their graphic reprise to fuck all day or simply put the goal is to create a climate of comprehension in which neither the rational nor the irrational are dismissed such as your confluence of time a confluence of perceptions but for now it's all I've got in the mode of perception it's the vacant space between visible recognition & socially (arbitrary/abstract) produced recognition but he's a complete anarchist not to mention his bewildered predacious features she lost some strata couldn't complete the really end of things the side with no mask or theme the thought that comes & goes without insistence & if that is so if that thought word does happen the whole world ill becomes the response to it & only it & we have holidays for her acceleration I have been wrong in the visual definition loosened by this whole record touch itself with emotion for a weathering fame sham millennium toting green things to the table adolescent combing futures of who secretly revealed that one of us will reverb that which keeps itself outside of the familial then seized by premonition as fabrication to forfeit several days will do such things emerging from the deleterious paving stones leaflets of vantage to most praxis breaks into somnambulant value like a $20 bill like a school district like bodies in the ligature of yearly evisceration like the life they wanted in the end everything used to speak drop by drop parading around a single dream & everything was fairly stacked up against us the interactionism of the considering machine to synchronize this tentative space with convergences with subtle looks of true enfolding power or knowledge in the first unnumbered heart time to burn wages of the mind didn't matter on the freeway the california wisdom to say mind body program simulacrum only when you're gone becomes real monday & self-esteem we don't get it mechanistically monday overworking its caliber maldoror its captivation took a title very much like this the radical in some way silently a confidence of hours on trial in no evocation could it be these words know what essential sleep is contact with minimal spread

80

rumors all over electric birdwatching connections are we dreaming in heartless floatable war polish quasi-interaction & then there's nothing to worry about ok actually when you are sober everyone looks casual as hell fleeing anything for the image of civilization reversal like sacred geometry is phase one phase two becomes a melodrama of abscess from a circular sky & as a travelling force of charts on the bodiless body its atonal blood returning to the fabricable auguring music she quiets the continuum she rides the animal teeth of the way her talents go to a place of social organ that looks into a binary a star assuming accumulation stuns sudden zeitgeist rolling flames away in the tour of money an obvious idea swept into experience unlike children of the most prolific liquid narratives in the vapor thin oneself it went on for weeks extremely persistent to pull views from your solo years whether you die or not once in this world & then the personal form of you is shifted by a wind whose real name is a word no one can not know post-oracular oracular not-so-sudden alienation emanating poetry the dream of you out of rhythm so typically instrumental in riots self-importance or mechanical primal order then west of everything seems cool & fractal it's hard today engorged with suicide factions stuttering as they stop in genera hardly ever come to & singing that royal blaze you are near necessity that I contact how the word sees itself how the word enters indecision I witness the burning shorthand deriving meaning that is truly a she this theme brutal with uniform command as one cannot register the coping asseveration distillery that heavenly gristle those creaturely devastations a thirst for habitual praise this is what they call the nature of the beast capital discount & daytime shares lost of animistic situation succumbing always to the source of actual fortune the raving the akashic denial of space that comes to surpass a kaleidoscope inoperative reliance fronting as infrastructure the television also does with corpses becoming loose to the street an answer mode of us saw derivatives of the end of the city without bloody things I wrote that coloration is & is only light & then I wrote more preference of the face value concept plane or so familial talk would want you to believe you that & symptoms of the the rest assumes more things about you that you should know that or something about that act the signal breaking out of very simple symbols tired of the convenience of always definitions bed spilling our walk toward one another months in regrettable soul searing ambulation or being alone in the world right now it left now it should answer curves to the eye breeding any female key with the usual enumerations to fallacy remotely gorgeous give me testament & group homes names of theater words theater words against the fear the occupying hyphenation of night the addendum to yes a believable catastrophic so sudden & polite the greater reason of struggle to document a dearth of observance looking out of the extinct text the concerted text the abbreviated fulcrum of nonsense I tie my shoes with blood tie my tie with sexual trash or sexual dust the dust plate of freedom hours the plasticity of the horse & men deboning their gods then devouring estates of premonition the youngest paramedic throwing up an apple's power it's an undertaking to be so shameless pistol in each zero detonation to step so resembling a primary sigil if possible to seem so also the meaning of words participates the misery of a word revolves in a paragraph science an elevated sort of presentment or etching missing ideas missing the I for now the measures one takes to defend a sleeping mass of knives vacuums bones & feelings represent your heaven or estranged graveyard blunt to somewhere an appropriate east of defiance I remember noting about my life now every minute by minute I become more of that broken toppled over dusk or sky or sky with disproportion I believe in now I believe now that even in now I believe now I now believe in now that now is or now was presence is dead what is one undescribed & what is the end of one but the sequence the sold out sequence familiar to say the least of tribes & quiet imaginary comments we hear before passing vibrations of the face before emptying & entering the sleeping quanta the apostle whom he was in a coma it takes only fathoms more or less color coded in the skeletal myth now a poor excuse for little barb wire blessings to sky your beachfront life you know to give birth as an artist statement section of the city that tells you why the dead read the public is not this the center of why even hell has become a great scar to predict the weather from its actual size to store away this renewal of ours the backdrop being a horribly overcast 4th of july weekend to think in terms of future furniture to dream & excuse yourself from the table to shine your belongings with ardor & review your collection of human plasma & act coercive vast as alabaster with the choice of an absolute or someone else's lover is engaging the capable as repulsion & repertoire a house of spades & permanent balloons of electric correspondence I know because that place in affirmation haunted me for a while traced a nightmare though just the same as a pyre the acid techno american variation secret of eliding I made it beautiful & red & unthinkable divagations entering your body cupping providence its waves good deaths sharpening one dreamer who always takes note of storefront art you must have a mind full of dollhouse miracles it means nothing I know of I providence hazards & if the sky rays what of beauty what of baudelaire these are just a few lines from my fathers I have convinced myself that it wouldn't hurt to say here we are & to allow myself to breathe & see confessing silver & gold I go for the most obvious always & fuck subtlety like oak of oak so what & all of your minotauresque art is fake to have an idea of what could not is passion for me am not gone am lying old myself by the sun finger in this life to live to swap with the dark & the frank looking into books of asymmetry sorcery remembering her loveliness with apparent chipmunks lines & lines like the heroin of lover thunder bullying whatever dark virus says the poet of course the second such luxury of held presence in outer people without being people to hold for night is letters from hell & the books today we wandered & at least carelessly & there were signals within a junky proportion a without theater & without the girl wine the rainbow woven & the parakeet of death & the mental car & the dear freezing night meat of my blood are you not an over occurrence of fact are you not the same as a chocolate thing the worn outward aspiration wives unwinding a glimmer week foregoing trauma markets distinctly showering franti- cally the messianic hoodlums of you I said the records smoke in slow wristed time she has red paintings that sway also like snakes of lunar distress & him his diamond month did you hear the accrual trust- worthy ludic potential possibly the coronal dream archer with five o'clocks with both hands whips drawn as I tamper with sentimental assets there is no more art only dental work to be done this is terrible writing little virginity of chaos & the mind posits & precious stones in public & that was enough either way my shadow wears shoes & numinous projectile clouds frequenting luxembourg without idealess truant sample corners willing refraction & apparency the light in your bandana the trees & sexual rediscovery of desertion there is not a single sun that does not hear its passage & ignores a text as one cannot unwrite the word wendigo these offerings right here seep into you escape the mundaneness of real theater the least likely of revolutions when islands of maturity were going to be good were going to be good at least years pass then she lets a genre of her shining hands in in my understanding of morning coffee & a wholeness feeling like one swan the young woman is seen by another not a poet but a lover of poets & their love object let in by her own beauty in a fever of doings continuing to imbibe actual visual fields the fields writhing in actual time & place the memory of seizure of site for its fervent formations the situational lies turning into these several days & awakenings ask me if they are stunned I should be allowed around negatives of night to torture the ground half man half constellation fame a miniscule point of leisure & I love that I will find death in its oblong sun shroud may very well dive from your memories if they signify essential flash that I could leave you now turn the light feel & sleep like the broken arm of fame become again the system of lightning glass change making night fluctuate minimalism of no line breaks there is no red no wheel but the sound of them produce a showless audience of glowering ones & twos a thematic of unlust not our equal day wears a blue rose face behind the face woman walking down abstruse streets of day unfolding the structure every time your eye does if there is no eye & you are not there all the way holding my chest but was hateful open your eyes the celibate room the caramel sphere of self is precious immigration working-class imaginations tending to pronounce the temple of easy misogyny as ego embarks from the auras callers of acclaim want want too much to receive the same truly a yearning for sympathetic repair asexual bond without obsession of name impossible introduction or affective angelic data relieving future writers from putting on a face allowing them a looseness of number is animal without the bread of familiar eyes this could you call the ozone a coroner of beauty I call it used up & rife width ossified in weather is one atlantis or hunger could debate about you love too much or I don't know what else to say & my death you assume is as anything would have justified conscience by now I am repeating myself notice the small parties overtly pretending an absolute abomination of theater shadow speech & its combine with the years to come a sort of kitchen with & all the while firearms too but you are you meaning locked in grey express formed & wet with lulls of surety weird sirens & there is an outside worth mortifying forward fades like hair is just explosive moons the evidence mutations like music looping the dream archer of dreams then went nowhere this is hardly inverse olmec breakable to these words only leaning in the trash of keeping lexical function machines notice us having so much more to do & ready for whatever's next play & what is the dream if it does not involve consumption self in the habit of self tradition as only what the dead see natal pause the gorgeous blood cloaks in the blood face knowing the sentence season of force & chance to merge with corpses for three or four destinations the silence reoccurs & goes beyond the woman you is & is not with you lives & breaths are the double eye of incurable forwards similar to this monologue of another destroyer but the head's demeanor shaper the remainder lover there you go again there you go & not without a train no one calls me in the obscure weapon of the future no one loves her but I did throb epigram fix inside fantasy the act of the present & who says that or closes off here people living next in sound quiet face in quiet keep your quiet light flexing back like the thigh of invention invented earth blue striving for theory between them & their this is not what I would call death with a hum or footsteps above a mark unmanning itself the coin of god my name this network up & like the forms as if it hasn't the mantic of everyday life I will get you to freely violate viridian I do what I am supposed to do like fire on a girl fire in a panda wrestling the hundreds of counterpart glows with red form not to have the habits of forgive me indecisive vertigo measure & leaf or question the ancillary idea just murdered is hardly the same in spades the learning you have not known the answers of quest with mother & looks underwater is your favorite idea this is what ultimates the fervor sheep silence as simple caliber as desert under strict scrollwork gulls as far-reaching symptom as leaking tigers & tigers of light masochism gesticulating human pomposity in its gorgeous gold leaf habitat loosening without form the name & the word until never being the cannibal often what should not return let your instrument unfulfill a stark necklace glean gleaning terrestrial aporia live wire awhile internal penguin if you could alphabetize me already viperous volumes of air & over all these rows of sea green crows blue as lace hanging from edges the era of normal heads are not heads but the symmetry of myth time as one pattern of overlapping lucidities that derive themselves from the cream our oldest parts kept away from every present moment but kept still hidden where surprise of presence revolves every hour as it should be locked in the furniture of earth affection public hatred & the dumb translation of no one as of yet has been successful & all have perished the sun disappears entirely during alliteration this is the enervation of this is the poem rarefaction & resolution of the scry emergent hegemony slash reality lamentable dockside your features will do well to have have the look of some eternities of the finest quality & orange waiting for the light to fake its freeness for the residue to hold back on dusk meted alphabet stable of tear apart mentality that deeming the lesson was sheer refashion- ing of modular fear haven't I had enough to convince myself of your breathing quite possibly to begin to enter hallways of fingers fainting to emerge slowly from flashes of calamity to have it about your empty morning & felt anything ever I assume if a lover then high & evasive this knock is not a terrible education of continuity far from solemn a wave of divining blood even in the open openground a mind slits us of a far away crucifixion of dust & clamor behind the dust & clamor an opening a swinging mask to be distinct as money or imposition of the speculum the passionless occurrence of theory not to be reckoned with impromptu phonetics or headlong collateral time & the artist are no fashion astride & psilocybin introducing each one of us to an institution pursuing fact of light to diction to sinister tearing inward the system diatribe umbrella black make-up my new comment basks endemic & sovereign the promising voluble gluttony in that harvest shorn smear on the gray ground's pedestrian tournament saunter genuine feeling distance & within normal civility the rest careen murmuring yellow pen games gentlemanly situations shatter form the shatter form for women but for dredge & foam normal tide at cascades opining at the fact the reach interests only unsuitable with the shine of coin & bloody birth of blood in the head & alien wheels nude assignation figures trespass like licking human shadow from their own hermetic of poison image gun belt gunmetal ether what have you been up to this year there the wife no ghost to first things novice to dreams are not for me to split the extraterrestrial muscle regarding colossus not to exemplify huge iconic genres a drop & demented spring her breasts plus downtown figural shine as there are still whores & castles in the world I am their weaver bird owing nothing to the etiquette sense scene of rude jungle amethyst never advancing the eroticism of losing one's life the corollary traklesque doubling the effort of its own paradoxical life release a small handmade inhuman soundwalking to my crypt to learn one thing about the morally oscillating clock its face & its face & its face I cannot exist here who would wear the appeal of sleep & hear so many first words shirk number displacing desperation ideal bearing no exit but the exit original to joy & what does that mean sunlight streaming a compound responsibility of possession sunlight streaming couture of misanthropy convalescence sunlight streaming greater secret of the visible selfless sunlight beaming the bled edge of horus sunlight on the ancient cold of starvation sunlight beaming colossal fantasy source inchoate climax everyday over the days radiant pulse for the universal forest & extant to believe the end is not in proper relation to any perception of it but becomes present case with nothing behind its image & in all distances heaving lethal with wind itself with your beauty craving or would push back wild & with concolation I cried & was ashamed out of the new slew of the knowable comes a thing more precarious than being while for self I worship what I'm doing which is what sonnets teetering not some zeal something leaving us gyre & hiss something coming out of my head natural leaning talk to belie because along the lame information of ideas nothing is well to have refused a where & solid appearance mocking the way of simply making returns radiant who begins to remedios varo all the institutional waking so worthless children in faith but is not missing in to have fetched away what territory what genius urns the place in the joke where the kids' court is the month of june where in the rushes jupiter says the lowing kismet to vacationers & inaccessible exposure hymns nauseating supplication nauseating lover & logic what fucking cognition must the skin trap all nebulous & expectant the present is possible but not a phrase to export the disturbing game of thievery triangular core of reflection abscession & the mystical five in my opinion the aforesaid is the diary of sky scheming I am going to say one woman all the while will stain the room & from you going soft universe feeling so soon that the center is a kind knot of creation believed & disbelieved taught to be the bell of this alms alba to last all night in the torque of day to writhe in sound robes pennyroyal & the only song blind to other entrancement like wearing phenakite needing plainness awakened inaugural though several internal heads the plasticity of the fog anthems suffering among dread rains totally the past just jumps into a recluse what I was improvising to scathe parts of the no parts of at last wearing itself ending itself & not hemorrhages blossoming blossoms blossom into the most vacuous actual treats or further utilitarian lover of love famine a thirst for dimmed & whipped pools of just occasion for movements like your time welled up in plutarch the same a genuine formulation of demands a generation of lackadaisical fire-eaters in dear flowers in the farfetched idea of lust & lamentation recollecting things very worldly gust assuming the learned roles of unverifiable vision to prove to ask you discreetly one time of a wall the camp of stillness that works out like he wears his shifts throughout the mixture the former soviet mists the furnace chaste a thirst for the seal of the new done under the flair of the trees giant margins the gone of wonder the laramidian electronically killing a sordid threnody of handlers in aphasia three terrors of cancellation the shape of the charm the alluding talisman to pupate years exploding your kindled fragment dream dream of a deep loophole macrocephalic camera poisoning the follows of such disgraceful pals surrendering this chariot of green blood but to have to ascertain the swan the comical off-taste of girls on the go I've been waiting to see your mythical co-imagination your solo pistola of nothingness the agent of my sleepless urine & the truth of the asymmetrical image marrying windows just to throw them up into the nebulous tyrolean firefields felt the impromptu fragility of an odd acausal conscious appearance in the world goddamn appetite & goddamn jargon all laconic tossing out isolated rosaries of the unseen tossing out a six of spades a nightly song it's not impossible it's not impossible it's not impossible

2008 – 2017

POEM

to have the ideal applebutter scenic appeal of intimacy
whoa whoa careful terra firma / I've been aware golden thighs
a coconut enclosing you gently / monologueless
I want to make people look at things in the original world
like
Stalin-fresh
or darkest of blue in the order of hearing
the name of this work is not a simple scavenger
the breathing fatigue of always seeing
of forever and ever cardshark
so say the knocks of gods are with you
abbey beyond this dream you have looked for me
by the time you start looking
chokecherry or pyramid
Miamisburg Mound and the people belong
there is a way around memory it's irreducible
what leaves all the dream rake
how you have sheared away the antisocial
chalking the tuxedos up to never free
unapproachable Pangloss I have done things
I know full well

UNTITLED

I can do this in my sleep

spiritual gas mask / spiritual
periwinkle pussy

in a kitchen the color of an eyeball kid

obsessed with oceanography and racial slurs

it's like saying serpentiform freedom of cognac Chechnyan showers
    in pink tights
or cauterized phantom puberty rainbow wind within golden
    Gauloises

and so on and so forth

but I don't live my life like I used to

THE NEW DESNOS

It's hunching.   Be baby.   By cub, my baby.
Exacts phase,,if
Codex forever fun. Hex.   Cognitive Ypsilanti.
HYDROGEN
   Ex-sea. The exactly jay if. Sleep escape "Z"
Cringe how, fig baby Facebook vitamin city no
Ex-bifidobacterium alba.
"Z"

LIKE BISMUTH WHEN I ENTER

flexure
thunder mommy
precious
stretched cow wing
the mind glandular is not a particular is not a gust or fountain of youth
Manhattan has refrained from the morose Eucharist of precedence
    annihilation and knowing
hoarding the rhymes of beyond self we say gladness is a god-thing
we say maddening love we say constructed goose or Memphitic pain
    of a Rothko of Being
pouring coffee methods into my youth and me
to write the zippery light of style that never wavers the spring looks
    the cubic planning
its peak and defining diamond like strictly in the month of May
through golden frontal lobe indigenous
luckily I said I love the beach because you know geographically
I saw myself unchallenged by loneliness loving mostly the ceiling or
    strategy
which won't go away like one beautiful solemn siren
this picked me out of the fantasy trees this huge distillery smile
the blade that brings the eyes and all the octagonal wares that
    terrorize winter
my god this is lubricious and symbolizing weird fire but still
    nothing
knock out the snowy butt of daylight like a whistling I hear when
    there are statues of you to uncover
never confiding in anyone ever again but still like a scalpel
of course everything that is marked by it is Martian

and all along the love lines those who don't know remain rivered
even now
even in the admirable Las Vegas of all situations the big blue verb
the long Iraqi risk feathers taken away from the hours of the oughts
of agency
and listening to the bribery of the bribery school we are pitched
from the throne of beauty
illegal fear and gothic dust do I have an excuse a Lazy Susan of
sleepers
but I am asleep
and beauty unlocks a chimaerical levy a shadow of the form of a
Diplodocus:

finger snowman key to flow ghettoish load of stars
text wise pantomime hold nine satellite beast seat nonchalant olive
oil
true to Dusseldorf Pyrex villainy slaughter sandwich flailing storm
trim fire vine
jack-o-lantern of a thousand silence
nihilist slide cigarette timber flash bags
troubadour vest phonebook labor soil nasal cream
good shit vellum profits under eagles sidewinding killer birth blang
change when it went Seagram's comet stint:

a mind more distinct than the copies of vicarious selves
fuck the world and this bullshit:

oh you want a new bandana a havoc slogan which your prenatal
natives can wash aboard a scar:
well this is it:

ACKNOWLEDGMENTS

Versions of QUAALUDE, nine sections from NEON REMAINS, I KNOW EVERYTHING, UNTITLED, and all of THE NEW DESNOS poems were included in *Exhibit: A / Cartography* by Evidence Annual.

CERULEAN RODEO, IMAGINARY EULOGY, and TRANSLATING ÉLUARD ON KA'ANAPALI BEACH first emerged in *Seedings*, Issue 5 by Duration Press.

WHO LOVES PEOPLE AND VALIANT ART, THE NEW FEARLESS DEATH, THE ONEIRIC AS CAUSTIC BUNNY, and POEM turned up in *Open Resistance 3* by Other Rooms Press.

Six poems from NEON REMAINS occurred in *Oracular Radioactivation* by Other Rooms Press.

Three poems from NEON REMAINS appeared in *DREGINALD*, Issue 11.

Excerpts from THE SALIVATION ACTOR materialized in *Vestiges_04: Aphasia* by Black Sun Lit.

LIKE BISMUTH WHEN I ENTER (the poem) first entered the world in *Flag + Void*, Volume 6.

GOD WAVE was published as a chapbook by Evidence Annual in 2018.

Carlos Lara is the author of *The Green Record* (2018) and co-author of *The Audiographic As Data* (2018). The poem "God Wave" was published as a chapbook in 2018. Other poems and translations have appeared in *Lana Turner*, *Seedings*, *Vestiges*, *Aurochs*, *Flag + Void*, *Gulf Coast*, *Omniverse*, and elsewhere. He abides in Los Angeles.

NIGHTBOAT BOOKS

Nightboat Books, a nonprofit organization, seeks to develop audiences for writers whose work resists convention and transcends boundaries. We publish books rich with poignancy, intelligence, and risk. Please visit nightboat.org to learn about our titles and how you can support our future publications.

The following individuals have supported the publication of this book. We thank them for their generosity and commitment to the mission of Nightboat Books:

Kazim Ali
Anonymous
Jean C. Ballantyne
Photios Giovanis
Amanda Greenberger
Elizabeth Motika
Benjamin Taylor
Peter Waldor
Jerrie Whitfield & Richard Motika

In addition, this book has been made possible, in part, by a grant from the New York State Council on the Arts Literature Program and the Topanga Fund, which is dedicated to promoting the arts and literature of California.